Contents

KU-645-293

Introduction

This is the play long known in the United States under the potentially misleading title of *The Good Woman of Sezuan*, and ever since its original publication there in 1948 as one of Brecht's *Two Parables for the Theatre* it has been closely linked with *The Caucasian Chalk Circle*. This is not just accidental, for up to a point the two plays share a common ancestry, in that both can be traced back to a fourteenth-century Chinese model – *The Chalk Circle* by Li Hsing-tao, which was adapted by the German poet Klabund in the early 1920s and staged by Max Reinhardt with great success in Berlin in 1924. Brecht himself was a friend of Klabund from Munich days, and had just become one of Reinhardt's junior directors. With *The Caucasian Chalk Circle* the connection is thus obvious; with *The Good Person of Szechwan* (for 'der gute Mensch' of the original title could be of either sex) it came through Friedrich Wolf's 'counter-play' *Tai Yang Wakes Up*, which was written as a modern corrective to the sentimental chinoiserie of Klabund's version, and which Piscator staged in 1932 in a simple didactic production that impressed Brecht. As a result both the Brecht plays have an oriental background – the one set in feudal times, the other modern – and use certain techniques of the Chinese theatre, such as the songs, the direct addressing of the audience, the wearing of masks and the almost gymnastic adaptability and virtuosity demanded of the actors. At the same time they stand out from his more didactic and politically committed works by being conceived as 'parables' – a description not previously used for his plays – and having ethical problems as their main concern. They tend to appeal to actors, impresarios and teachers who are nervous of the youthful cynicism and mature communism of Brecht's previous work, and would like a little more colour on their stage.

However, whereas *The Caucasian Chalk Circle* was written in California, with a view to Broadway production, the main work on *The Good Person of Szechwan* had begun earlier, shortly before he left Denmark in spring 1939, some six months before the outbreak of the Second World War. He was then preparing to move on to America as soon as the family could get visas, and no doubt he had started to think of the play's potentialities in the new world, even though there is no evidence of his having discussed them as he did in the case of *Galileo*. Certainly it was one of the four plays which he thought best suited for American production once he had arrived there, the others being *Galileo*, *Arturo Ui* and *Fear and Misery of the Third Reich*. It had however been a much more difficult play than any of these to write, and this may well have been due to the fact that it had started life in the first place as an idea for a play about Berlin, with no oriental references at all. More than once in his journal he complains about its complicated history: conceived some ten years before he began serious work on it, then worked on successively in Denmark, Sweden and Finland till he reluctantly undertook a last revision at the beginning of 1941, it seemed entirely concluded to him, and in the event he was never able to give it the final test by staging it under his own direction. At bottom the problem was how to maintain the original social point when the Chinese setting risked becoming (as he noted in mid–1940) a 'mere disguise, and a ragged disguise at that'. For the short play which he had sketched in 1930 as *Die Ware Liebe* (a pun roughly equivalent to 'Love is the Goods') was on a theme close to that of his story 'The Job' (*Short Stories 1921–1946*, p.112): a society where women's role was to be sold, but salesmen had to be men. This, rather than the ambiguities of good and evil, is what suggested that the Person should be a whore.

Just when Brecht first thought of locating the play in China we do not know, but it must have been at some point between the production of *Tai Yang Wakes Up* (whose influence can be seen in the factory scene and in some aspects of the role of Shen Teh) and the first reference to it in his journal for March 1939, by which time it was already an unfinished fragment consisting of five scenes under its present title. 'A thin structure of steel', he called it, and clearly he did not wish it to have an exotic flavour:

> the girl must be a big powerful person. the city must be a big, dusty uninhabitable place. [. . .] some attention must be paid to countering the risk of chinoiserie. the vision is of a chinese city's outskirts with cement works and so on. there are still gods around but aeroplanes have come in. perhaps the lover should be an unemployed pilot?

Repeatedly he seems to have become uneasy about the local colour and the degree of realism needed: was Shen Teh, for instance, to give her impoverished neighbours bread, or milk, or rice? Originally a vague name for the city, Szechwan itself, which is more properly the name of a province, became specified in the stage directions as 'The capital of Szechwan, which has been semi-europeanised'. This would-be precision, which contrasts oddly with his later insistence that Szechwan stands indifferently for 'all those places where man is exploited by man', is less vivid in the end than some of Brecht's wilder flights of geographical fantasy, for instance in *Man equals Man*. Even then his use of Chinese theatrical techniques had to be accentuated during the last laborious revisions before the play was duplicated. This was done so as to 'add a poetic element', making it lighter and more entertaining in an effort to make up for its undue length.

*   *   *

Duplicated scripts went off early in 1941 to Piscator and Kurt Weill in the United States, as well as to recipients in Sweden and Switzerland, the latter including the Zurich Schauspielhaus, who were even then preparing the world première of *Mother Courage*. Piscator seems to have been the first to react, and within a few weeks of Brecht's arrival in California on 21 July 1941 he responded enthusiastically, saying that he had begun negotiating about a possible production with the Theatre Guild; moreover the poet John Latouche, author of the patriotic-progressive 'Ballad for Americans', was interested in translating the play. Brecht however was not prepared to be hurried, preferring to wait until he knew whether he himself would be coming to New York, and meanwhile suggesting to Piscator that *Arturo Ui* would be a simpler play to mount. Whether he had already heard about the productions of Piscator's Dramatic Workshop at the New School is not clear, but they had featured a version of the Klabund *Chalk Circle* that March starring Dolly Haas (of *Broken Blossoms* fame) as the heroine, a performance which the *New York Post* praised for its 'quaintness and delicacy'; and soon the poet Hoffman Hays was warning Brecht that Piscator's errors of judgement might harm him with the Guild. It may have been as a result of this that he now began looking elsewhere for the possibility of a production, showing the script to Elisabeth Bergner, who knew his work from Munich and Berlin and was predisposed to help. Not only had she had one of her great successes in Klabund's play in 1924, but she now learned from Brecht that he had written *The Good Person* specifically for her to act (though all the early scripts carry a dedication to Helene Weigel), and what she heard of its story clearly intrigued her. On reading it however she found it boring and guessed that others would as well, while the film actress Anna May Wong – yet another who had acted in the Klabund play, this time in London in 1931 – seems to have lost interest after a first meeting in Hollywood engineered by Alexander Granach, another of Brecht's Berlin friends.

The sole effect of these approaches to actresses, then, was to enrage

Piscator, who saw that he was being neglected and by-passed and felt that this was a poor reward for all his efforts to get Brecht invited to the United States in the first place. Thereafter nothing more appears to have been heard from the Theatre Guild, and it looks as if Brecht then shunted the play into the sidings while he concentrated on the writing of Fritz Lang's Czech resistance film *Hangmen Also Die*. One night in August 1942 however his old friend the novelist Lion Feuchtwanger telephoned to say that he had heard from Zurich that the Schauspielhaus there wanted to produce the script which Brecht had sent them before leaving Europe. This decision came at a crucial turning point in the military fortunes of the Allies, shortly before the victories of Alamein and Stalingrad, and from then on Zurich became for some years Brecht's European base. Naturally he was not yet able to see any productions there, let alone to exert any kind of influence on the interpretation of his plays, and it is difficult even now to judge how far the committedly anti-Nazi Schauspielhaus company managed to grasp all his ideas. A recent academic essay (in Jan Knopf's version of Hecht's Suhrkamp 'Materialien' compilation) seizes on differences between the communist actors' 'fraction' and Leonard Steckel, the former Piscator actor who directed, to justify its writer's dismissal of the premiere on 4 February 1943 as a 'falsification' of the play. This is hardly the impression given by the contemporary review in *Die Tat*, which argues that all Brecht's devices worked, that the play was profoundly if unobtrusively political and that 'its characters could just as well be peasants and workers of our own country as Chinese ancestral portraits'. At all events its initial reception, unlike that of *Mother Courage* and (later) *Puntila*, never led Brecht to make any corrective changes to the text, which accordingly became the authorised version as we now have it.

And yet within a matter of weeks Brecht was planning a major rewrite which was to lead – as later in the case of *Galileo* – to the making of a shorter, tighter and in some ways stronger 'version for here', i.e. for the American stage. This originated in Kurt Weill's reaction to the script that Brecht had sent him, which the now successful composer wanted to make into a (presumably musical) play for Broadway production. During his long visit to New York (February to May inclusive) Brecht therefore spent a week with the Weills, establishing the outline given on pp. 121-6 of our notes. This, it seems, was to form the basis for a production to be set up some while after that of the *Schweik* musical which they were planning at the same time and hoped to have ready by the autumn. The full script must then have been written during the summer of 1943, after the completion of *Schweik in the Second World*

War: typed by Brecht, it is headed '1943 version' and datelined 'Santa Monica 1943'. It eliminates two scenes and five characters and is roughly two-thirds of the length of the Zurich (authorised) version; a note by Brecht suggests that only one copy exists; though unpublished in German it can be reconstructed from the passages quoted on pp. 132-48. Probably this is the version which Brecht gave Christopher Isherwood to read that September in the hope that he might translate it; however, only 'a few polite compliments' resulted. Weill anyway wanted a more radical adaptation by an American writer, possibly the black poet Langston Hughes, who later wrote the adaptation of *Street Scene* for him. By November it seems that the new Brecht version had been shelved, and that winter a contract was made giving Weill the right to choose his own librettist and lyric writer, along with exclusive production rights for the next two and a half years. By then he had come round to the idea of a 'semi-opera', in the term which he had used of *Silver Lake* in 1933, with its separate musical 'numbers'. (He never entirely abandoned the idea, but the work had still not been started when he died in 1950.)

For at least a year Weill's interest put a stopper on any further production plans, and although Brecht speculated to Leo Kerz about the possibility of setting the play in Jamaica with an all black cast (and a translation by Auden) it never rose to the surface of his concerns again until he left America for Switzerland in November 1947. It was only after that point that a wave of American college and university productions began, using the *Two Parables* translation which Eric and Maya Bentley had made at Brecht's request on the basis of the 1940 text. Perhaps it was this that once again aroused Broadway's interest, but by now Brecht was quite as reluctant to commit himself as he had been in the case of Piscator and the Theatre Guild. In particular he did not want any experimental productions in New York; Shen Teh must be played by 'an artiste of the first rank' (Jessica Tandy for example); while Bentley himself should not venture to direct in 'the hopeless atmosphere of Broadway' without first gaining experience with Brecht's own company in Berlin. As a result it was only after the writer's death in August 1956 that the play finally reached New York, when T.E. Hambleton put on a production that December at the Phoenix Theatre, directed by Bentley with Uta Hagen as Shen Teh. Two months earlier George Devine had staged it at the Royal Court Theatre in London with Peggy Ashcroft, after visiting Brecht earlier in the year and gaining his approval. Both these first productions had music by Paul Dessau and sets by Teo Otto, friends and accepted interpreters of Brecht.

How highly did Brecht himself rank the play? Certainly he never gave it a particularly high priority where German productions were concerned. Indeed the Berliner Ensemble itself were not to stage it until more than a year after his death. This was partly because of the considerable backlog of his plays which had either not been staged at all or not staged with his involvement and to his satisfaction. There was just too much to be done, particularly in view of the Ensemble's long drawn-out rehearsals and discussions. But it does seem also that Brecht still regarded *The Good Person* as an unusually difficult play to deal with, for all the apparent ease of its acceptance at college level. Nor were matters helped by the fact that its first professional postwar production was licensed and prepared without his being consulted; indeed the Brecht literature generally ignores it. This took place at Max Reinhardt's former Vienna theatre, the eighteenth-century Theater in der Josefstadt, where there was a production by Rudolf Steinböck in March 1946 with the outstanding actress Paula Wessely as Shen Teh; conservative Austrian critics felt she was too cold. It was another six years before Harry Buckwitz in Frankfurt mounted the first West German production, a somewhat dragging affair with Solveig Thomas as a clearly much sweeter and daintier Shen Teh. A number of other West German performances followed before Brecht, who had spent four days with Buckwitz in Frankfurt trying 'to infuse ease and clarity into the production', gave his young Swiss assistant Benno Besson the task of directing the play's East German première at Rostock. With Käthe Reichel as a dialectically polarised Shen Teh this laboured the play's antitheses and stressed the links between the Chinese city and Western capitalism. It was conceived as a pilot production for Besson and Reichel to develop eighteen months later at the Berliner Ensemble.

*   *   *

Despite its obvious attractions *The Good Person of Szechwan* is made up of too many conflicting layers simply to convey the thin steely strength or the clarity and ease for which Brecht variously aimed. Nor is there any evidence – either recorded or in the theatre-going memory – that it ever achieved one of the great Brecht productions, something to rank with the original *Threepenny Opera* and *The Mother*, the 1931 *Man equals Man*, the Hollywood *Galileo*, the Brecht/Engel *Mother Courage* and the Palitzsch/Wekwerth *Arturo Ui*. Not all those plays differed from it in the ease of their writing, both *Galileo* and *Man equals Man* being the product of many years of reconsideration and revision. The difficulty is rather that despite Brecht's warnings against a fancy-dress orientalising approach there is some danger of sentimentality and prettification in the play as he left it to us; indeed the example of the *Chalk Circle* (or *Circle of Chalk* in James Laver's 1931 translation) is hard to shake off. Perhaps because of this the actresses who have been tempted to play Shen Teh – even, it seems, when Brecht himself did the tempting – have started with an idealised model of the oriental 'good woman' before them, an image only slightly spiced up by her description as a prostitute. At the same time the social relevance of the original *Love is the Goods* story is not so much 'alienated' by the Szechwan setting as diffused and diluted by it. 'We had in mind a sort of golden myth' says the speaker of the epilogue, and this comforting interpretation is now available from the first appearance of the three hopelessly unserious gods.

Obviously Brecht in this play was concerned with something more than sharp formulations of the 'Food is the first thing. Morals follow on' variety. Not only had he been reading Chinese philosophy, but his journal shows that he had begun holding discussions about Marxist ethics with the actor Hermann Greid and other friends. In the *Flüchtlingsgespräche* or *Conversations between Exiles*, which he was writing in Finland around the same time, he deals with the concepts of good and evil in a comic-paradoxical way, showing in a long 'Parade of the Vices and Virtues' how both these opposites can 'identify themselves as the servants of *Oppression*'. The play however is more schematic, as may be seem from Brecht's notes on pp. 118-20. Moreover it is dialectical rather than paradoxical, and by splitting the central character down the middle into two irreconcilable parts it can easily cut away the point, which is that in aggressive and unjust societies good can only survive by means of evil. Nor is it ever made clear enough that the roof of this ethical duplicity is not simply poverty, such as can afflict any form of society; indeed only the 'Song of Green Cheese' at the end of scene 6 suggests that a better society can be conceived at all, and it does so in the most unreal fairy-story terms. Brecht, in other words, had only himself to blame if audiences applauded him for modifying his previously 'political' approach, and instead tackling the eternal problem of 'humanity as such'. The feeling with which they are most likely to be left by the play is one of generalised discontent.

Such problems of focus are built into *The Good Person of Szechwan*, and it could accordingly be argued that a faithful production is one that simply allows them to emerge. There are however ways of blocking some of the dangers against which Brecht warned us: by casting a 'big, powerful' Shen Teh for instance, or by eliminating the Chinese setting altogether as did Giorgio Strehler, who in his 1981 Milan production dropped it in favour of an Italian shanty town with filthy puddles everywhere. What seems rather surprising, in view of the high risk of having Shen Teh interpreted as a sweet-natured oriental waif, is that Brecht's experience of Chinese acting, which so influenced him in other respects, never led him to propose giving the dual role to a man. This would instantly correct any undue softness that may stem from the sexually loaded 'good woman' image; moreover it seems to make it easier to see elements of Shui Ta in Shen Teh and vice versa, as the parable surely demands; nor is there anything in the text to rule it out. Brecht, it is true, spoke of the part from the first as being 'for a woman', but this, like her designation as a prostitute, is traceable back to the original pre–1933 story. It is not specifically demanded by the 1940 play.

It is stranger still that the 'Americanised' version of 1943 has remained so little known, not even being considered in the 'Materialien' booklets or any of the standard Brecht literature except our Random House edition of the collected plays. For it is both tougher and more topically relevant to our societies today, in that the 'tobacco' in the sacks which the visiting family of scene 1 leave in Shen Teh's shop turns out to be opium. What is more, Shen Teh's evident complicity in this traffic, once Shui Ta begins selling the stuff, makes the good person's dependence on evil actions seem that much more real and less schematic. At the same time the puzzling financial complexities of the old people's loan, the highly improbable blank cheque from the barber and the proceeds of the sale both of the tobacco and the shop, which in the 1940 version were too much for Brecht ever to straighten out convincingly, are greatly simplified by the elimination of both loan and cheque: a definite gain. This generally faster-moving version was used in David Thompson's Greenwich Theatre production of May 1977 and gave a much clearer line to the story, though at the cost of losing two individually effective scenes: the wedding in the restaurant and the factory scene with its brutal 'Song of the Eighth Elephant'. In particular Sun, by ending up as an enfeebled addict, is much more convincingly 'broken-down' than the bowler-hatted 'charming manager' of the standard text.

Yet even here, a little archaeological excavation reveals a deeply buried foundation for the parable's new harshness. For the 'Song of the Smoke', which Brecht added to scene 1 as one of the last Finnish revisions, was derived from the three-part 'Song of the Opium Den' written about 1920; this is printed on pp. 111-112. Perhaps then the notion of drug addiction already hung faintly about the play underneath the grey cloud of twisting tobacco smoke which in the end came to determine its atmosphere. Such smoke, to Brecht, had an almost ritual quality; he associated it with the calm reflectiveness of the theatre audience or, as in the poem 'Pipes', of the political refugee waiting to be arrested. In the *Conversations between Exiles* the starting point is the low quality of the Finnish beer and cigars, the latter being something that the author ranked among his 'means of production'. In *Mother Courage*, whose writing interrupted that of *The Good Person*, Courage appreciates the Cook's character from the teeth marks on his pipe, while Yvette the whore first sings of him as 'Pipe and Drum Henny', then in the final version calls him 'Puffing Piet, cause he never took his pipe out of his mouth when he was on the job', an image derived perhaps from 'Surabaya Johnny' which led Ernst Busch as the Cook to insinuate a Dutch song about pipes into the Berliner Ensemble's script. All such echoes and overtones vanish once the Good Person's tobacco is changed back into a drug. A certain cosiness leaves this naturally likeable play as the black smoke takes over. Could the same disturbing effect be achieved with the tobacco imagery of 1940, presented with today's new awareness of its cancerous implications?

THE EDITORS

The Good Person of Szechwan
A parable play

COLLABORATORS: R. Berlau and M. Steffin

MUSIC: Paul Dessau

TRANSLATOR: John Willett

Written in 1938-41. First produced in the Zürich Schauspielhaus on 4 February 1943

CHARACTERS

Wang, a water-seller: Shen Teh-Shui Ta: Yang Sun, an unemployed airman: Mrs Yang, his mother: Mrs Shin, a widow: the family of eight: Lin To, a carpenter: Mrs Mi Tzu, a property owner: the policeman: the carpet-dealer and his wife: the young prostitute: Shu Fu, the barber: the priest: the unemployed man: the waiter: passers-by of the Prologue.

PROLOGUE

A Street in the Capital of Szechwan

It is evening. Wang, the water-seller, introduces himself to the audience.

WANG: I am a water-seller in the capital of Szechwan province. My job is tedious. When water is short I have to go far for it. And when it is plentiful I earn nothing. But utter poverty is the rule in our province. All agree that only the gods can help us. To my inexpressible joy a widely-travelled cattle dealer has told me that some of the highest gods are already on their way, and that Szechwan may see them too. They say that the heavens are deeply disturbed by the many complaints that have been going up. For the last three days I have waited at this entrance to the city, especially towards evening, so that I may be the first to greet them. There will hardly be a chance for me later; they will be surrounded by important people and there will be far too many demands on them. But shall I be able to recognise them? They may not arrive in a group. Perhaps they will come singly, so as not to attract attention. It cannot be those men – *he studies some workmen passing by* – they are coming away from work. Their shoulders are bent by the burdens they have to carry. That fellow is no god either, he has inky fingers. At most he may be some kind of clerk in a cement works. I would not take those gentlemen – *two gentlemen walk past* – for gods even: they have the brutal faces of men who beat people, and the gods find that unnecessary. But look at these three! They seem very different. They are well nourished, show no evidence of any kind of employment, and have dust on their shoes, so they must have travelled far. It is them! Yours to command, Illustrious Ones!

He flings himself to the ground.

THE FIRST GOD, *pleased*: Have you been expecting us?

WANG *gives them a drink*: For a long while. But only I knew that you were coming.

THE FIRST GOD: We must find a lodging for tonight. Do you know of one?

WANG: One? Lots! The city is at your service, O Illustrious Ones. Where do you wish to stay?

The gods exchange significant looks.

THE FIRST GOD: Try the first house, my son. Take the very first one first.

WANG: I only fear that I may attract the enmity of the powerful, if I give one of them the preference.

THE FIRST GOD: Then take it as an order: try the first one.

WANG: That's Mr Fo opposite. One moment.

He runs to a house and hammers on the door. It opens, but one can see him being turned away. He comes hesitantly back.

WANG: How stupid. Mr Fo happens to be out just now, and his servants dare not take the responsibility, as he is very strict. Won't he be angry when he finds who has been turned away!

THE GODS, *smiling*: Indeed.

WANG: Another moment then! The house next door is the widow Su's. She will be beside herself with joy.

He runs there, but is apparently turned away once more.

I shall have to ask across the road. She says she has only one very small room, and it's in no fit state. I will go straight to Mr Cheng's.

THE SECOND GOD: But a small room is all we need. Tell her that we are coming.

WANG: Even if it has not been cleaned? Suppose it is crawling with spiders?

THE SECOND GOD: No matter. The more spiders, the fewer flies.

THE THIRD GOD, *in an amiable way*: Try Mr Cheng or anybody else you like, my son. I admit I find spiders a little un-attractive.

Wang knocks at another door and is admitted.

A VOICE FROM THE HOUSE: Get away with your gods! We've got enough troubles of our own.

WANG, *returning to the gods*: Mr Cheng is extremely sorry, he has his whole house full of relatives and dare not appear before you, Illustrious Ones. Between ourselves, I think there are evil men among them whom he would prefer you not to see. He is much too frightened of your judgment. That must be it.

THE THIRD GOD: Are we all that frightening?

WANG: Only to evil people, isn't it? We all know that Kwan province has suffered from floods for years.

THE SECOND GOD: Oh? And why is that?

WANG: Because they are not god-fearing people, I suppose.

THE SECOND GOD: Rubbish. Because they didn't look after the dam properly.

THE FIRST GOD: Sh! *To Wang*: Any other prospects, my son?

WANG: How can you ask? I have only to go to the next house, and I can have my pick. They are all falling over each other to entertain you. An unlucky combination of circumstances, you understand. Half a minute.

He walks away hesitantly and stands in the street unable to make up his mind.

THE SECOND GOD: What did I tell you?

THE THIRD GOD: It may just be circumstances.

THE SECOND GOD: Circumstances in Shun, circumstances in Kwan, and now circumstances in Szechwan. There are no god-fearing people left: that is the naked truth which you will not recognize. Our mission is hopeless, and you had better admit it.

THE FIRST GOD: We may still come across good people at any moment. We cannot expect to have things all our own way.

THE THIRD GOD: The resolution says: the world can go on as it is if we find enough good people, able to lead a decent human existence. The water-seller himself is such a person, if I am not deceived.

He goes up to Wang, who is still standing uncertain.

THE SECOND GOD: He is always deceived. When the water man let us drink out of his measure I saw something. Look.

He shows it to the first god.

THE FIRST GOD: It has got a false bottom.
THE SECOND GOD: A swindler.
THE FIRST GOD: Very well, we strike him out. But what does it matter if one man is corrupted? We shall soon find plenty who fulfil the conditions. We must find someone. For two thousand years we have been hearing the same complaint, that the world cannot go on as it is. No one can stay on earth and remain good. We must at last be able to show some people who are in a position to keep our commandments.
THE THIRD GOD, *to Wang*: Is it too difficult for you to find us a place?
WANG: Such guests as you? What are you thinking of? It is my fault that you were not taken in immediately; I am a bad guide.
THE THIRD GOD: Not that, certainly.

He turns back to the others.

WANG: They have begun to realise. *He accosts a gentleman*: Honoured sir, forgive me for addressing you, but three of the highest gods, whose impending advent has been the talk of all Szechwan for years, have now really arrived and are looking for a place to spend the night. Don't walk away. Look for yourself. One glance will convince you. For heaven's sake do something about it. It's the chance of a lifetime! Invite the gods to visit your home before someone else snaps them up; they are sure to accept.

The gentleman has walked on. Wang turns to another.

You, sir, you heard what it's about. Have you any room? It needn't be palatial. The intention is what matters.

THE GENTLEMAN: How am I to tell what sort of gods yours are? Heaven knows who I might be letting into my house.

He goes into a tobacconist's. Wang runs back to the three.

WANG: I have found somebody who is sure to take you.

He sees his measure on the ground, looks embarrassedly at the gods, picks it up and runs back again.

THE FIRST GOD: That does not sound encouraging.

WANG, *as the man steps out of the shop*: What about the accommodation?

THE GENTLEMAN: How do you know I'm not living in rooms myself?

THE FIRST GOD: He will find nothing. We had better write Szechwan off too.

WANG: It's three of the chief gods. Truly. Their images in the temples are just like them. If you get your invitation in now they might perhaps accept.

THE GENTLEMAN *laughs*: I suppose they're a lot of prize swindlers you're trying to foist off on someone.

Off.

WANG, *shouting after him*: You swivel-eyed chiseller! Have you no reverence? You'll all roast in brimstone for your lack of interest. The gods crap on the lot of you. And you'll be sorry for it. You shall pay for it unto the fourth generation. You have disgraced the whole province. *Pause.* That leaves us with Shen Teh the prostitute; she can't refuse.

He calls 'Shen Teh!' Shen Teh looks out of the window above.

They've arrived, and I can't find them a room. Could you possibly have them for one night?

SHEN TEH: Not much hope, Wang. I am expecting someone. But how is it that you can't find a room for them?

WANG: I can't explain now. Szechwan is nothing but one big muck-heap.

SHEN TEH: I should have to hide when he arrives. Then he might go away. He was supposed to be taking me out.

WANG: Can we come up in the meantime?

SHEN TEH: If you don't talk too loudly. Do I have to be careful what I say?

WANG: Very. They mustn't find out how you earn your living. We had better wait downstairs. But you won't be going off with him, will you?

SHEN TEH: I've had no luck lately, and if I can't find the rent by tomorrow they'll throw me out.

WANG: You shouldn't think of money at a moment like this.

SHEN TEH: I don't know: I'm afraid that a rumbling stomach is no respecter of persons. But very well, I will take them in.

She is seen to put out her light.

THE FIRST GOD: It looks hopeless to me.

They go up to Wang.

WANG, *startled to see them standing behind him*: You are fixed up for the night.

He wipes the sweat off his face.

THE GODS: Really? Then let us go.

WANG: There is no great hurry. Take your time. The room is not quite ready.

THE THIRD GOD: Very good, we will sit here and wait.

WANG: But isn't there too much traffic here? Let's cross the road.

THE SECOND GOD: We like looking at people. That is exactly what we came for.

WANG: It's a windy spot.

THE THIRD GOD: Does this seem all right to you?

They sit on a doorstep. Wang sits on the ground somewhat to one side.

WANG, *with a rush*: You are lodging with a girl who lives on her own. She is the best person in Szechwan.

THE THIRD GOD: That is gratifying.

WANG, *to the audience*: When I picked up my mug just then they gave me a peculiar look. Do you think they noticed anything? I daren't look them in the face any longer.

THE THIRD GOD: You seem exhausted.

WANG: A little. I have been running.

THE FIRST GOD: Do people here find life very hard?

WANG: Good people do.

THE FIRST GOD, *seriously*: Do you?

WANG: I know what you mean. I am not good. But I too find life hard.

Meanwhile a gentleman has appeared in front of Shen Teh's house and whistled a number of times. Each time Wang gives a nervous jerk.

THE THIRD GOD, *in an undertone to Wang*: It looks as if he has given up.

WANG, *confused*: It does.

He jumps up and runs into the open, leaving his carrying-pole behind. But the following has occurred: the man waiting has gone off and Shen Teh, after opening the door quietly and calling 'Wang!' in a low voice, has gone down the street in search of Wang. When Wang in turn calls 'Shen Teh!' in a low voice he gets no reply.

WANG: She has let me down. She has gone off to get the money for the rent, and I have no place for the Illustrious Ones. They are waiting there, exhausted. I cannot go back yet again and tell them: no good, sorry. My own sleeping place under the culvert is out of the question. And I am sure the gods would not care to lodge with a man whose dirty business they have seen through. I would not go back for anything in the world. But my carrying-pole is still there. What shall I do? I dare not fetch it. I shall leave the capital and find somewhere where I can hide from their eyes, for I failed to do anything to help those I honour.

He hurries away. As soon as he has gone, Shen Teh returns, searches for him on the opposite side and sees the gods.

SHEN TEH: Are you the Illustrious Ones? My name is Shen Teh.
    I should be happy if you consented to make do with my small
    room.

THE THIRD GOD: But where has the water-seller disappeared to?

SHEN TEH: I must have missed him.

THE FIRST GOD: He probably thought you were not coming,
    and then felt too scared to come back to us.

THE THIRD GOD *picks up the carrying-pole*: We will ask you to
    look after it. He needs it.

*They enter the house led by Shen Teh. It grows dusk, then light
again. In the half-light of the dawn the gods again leave the door,
led by Shen Teh guiding them with a lantern. They take their leave.*

THE FIRST GOD: Dear Shen Teh, we are grateful for your hospi-
    tality. We shall not forget that it was you who took us in.
    Will you give the water-seller his pole back? And tell him
    that we are grateful to him too for having shown us a good
    person.

SHEN TEH: I am not good. I have an admission to make: when
    Wang asked me if I could shelter you I had hesitations.

THE FIRST GOD: Hesitations do not count if you overcome them.
    Know that you gave us more than a lodging. There are many,
    including even certain of us gods, who have begun to doubt
    whether such a thing as a good person still exists. To check
    up was the main object of our journey. We are now happy
    to continue it, for we have succeeded in finding one. Farewell.

SHEN TEH: Wait, Illustrious Ones. I am by no means sure that
    I am good. I should certainly like to be, but how am I to pay
    the rent? Let me admit: I sell myself in order to live, and
    even so I cannot manage, for there are so many forced to do
    this. I would take on anything, but who would not? Of course
    I should like to obey the commandments: to honour my
    parents and respect the truth. Not to covet my neighbour's
    house would be a joy to me, and to love, honour and cherish
    a husband would be very pleasant. Nor do I wish to exploit
    other men or to rob the defenceless. But how can it be done?

Even by breaking one or two of the commandments I can barely manage.

THE FIRST GOD: All these, Shen Teh, are but the doubts of a good person.

THE THIRD GOD: Goodbye, Shen Teh. And give our warmest greetings to the water-seller. He was a good friend to us.

THE SECOND GOD: I fear we did but little good to him.

THE THIRD GOD: The best of luck.

THE FIRST GOD: Above all, be good, Shen Teh. Goodbye.

They turn to go. They begin to wave goodbye.

SHEN TEH, *nervously*: But I am not certain of myself, Illustrious Ones. How can I be good when everything is so expensive?

THE SECOND GOD: Alas, that is beyond our powers. We cannot meddle in the sphere of economics.

THE THIRD GOD: Wait! Just a minute. If she were better provided she might stand more chance.

THE SECOND GOD: We cannot give her anything. We could not answer for it up there.

THE FIRST GOD: Why not?

They put their heads together and confer animatedly.

THE FIRST GOD, *awkwardly, to Shen Teh*: We understand that you have no money for the rent. We are not poor people, so it is natural that we should pay for our lodging. Here you are. *He gives her money.* But please let nobody know that we paid. It might be misinterpreted.

THE SECOND GOD: Only too easily.

THE THIRD GOD: No, it is permissible. We can quite well pay for our lodging. There was nothing against it in the resolution. So fare you well.

The gods exeunt rapidly.

I

A small Tobacconist's

The shop is not yet properly installed, and not yet open.

SHEN TEH, *to the audience*: It is now three days since the gods left. They told me they wanted to pay for their lodging. And when I looked at what they had given me I saw that it was more than a thousand silver dollars. I have used the money to buy a tobacconist's business. I moved in here yesterday, and now I hope to be able to do a great deal of good. Look at Mrs Shin, for instance, the old owner of the shop. Yesterday she came to ask for rice for her children. And today I again see her bringing her pot across the square.

Enter Mrs Shin. The women bow to one another.

SHEN TEH: Good evening, Mrs Shin.

MRS SHIN: Good evening, Miss Shen Teh. What do you think of your new home?

SHEN TEH: I like it. How did the children spend the night?

MRS SHIN: Oh, in someone's house, if you can call that shack a house. The baby's started coughing.

SHEN TEH: That's bad.

MRS SHIN: You don't know what's bad. You've got it good. But you'll find plenty to learn in a dump like this. The whole district's a slum.

SHEN TEH: That is right what you told me, though? That the cement workers call in here at midday?

MRS SHIN: But not a customer otherwise, not even the locals.

SHEN TEH: You didn't tell me that when you sold me the business.

MRS SHIN: That's right: throw it in my face. First you take the roof away over the children's heads, and then it's nothing but dump and slum. It's more than I can bear.

She weeps.

SHEN TEH, *quickly*: I'll get your rice.

MRS SHIN: I was going to ask you if you could lend me some money.

SHEN TEH, *as she pours rice into her bowl*: I can't do that. I haven't sold anything yet.

MRS SHIN: But I need it. What am I to live on? You've taken everything I've got. Now you're cutting my throat. I'll leave my children on your door-step, you bloodsucker!

She snatches the pot from her hands.

SHEN TEH: Don't be so bad-tempered. You'll spill your rice.

Enter an elderly couple and a shabbily dressed man.

THE WOMAN: Ah, Shen Teh, my dear, we heard you were doing so nicely now. Why, you've set up in business! Just fancy, we're without a home. Our tobacconist's shop has folded up. We wondered if we mightn't spend a night with you. You know my nephew? He can't abide being separated from us.

THE NEPHEW, *looking round*: Smashing shop.

MRS SHIN: Who's this lot?

SHEN TEH: When I arrived here from the country they were my first landlords. *To the audience*: When my small funds ran out they threw me on the street. They are probably frightened that I will say no. They are poor.

> They have no shelter.
> They have no friends.
> They need someone.
> How can they be refused?

Addressing the woman in a friendly voice: Welcome to you, I will gladly give you lodging. But all I have is a tiny room at the back of the shop.

THE MAN: That'll do us. Don't you worry. *While Shen Teh fetches them tea*: We'd better move in behind here, so as not to be in your way. I suppose you picked on a tobacconist's to remind you of your first home? We'll be able to give you one or two tips. That's another reason for coming to you.

MRS SHIN, *sardonically*: Let's hope one or two customers come too.

THE WOMAN: Is that meant for us?

THE MAN: Sh. Here's a customer already.

Enter a tattered man.

THE UNEMPLOYED MAN: Excuse me, miss, I'm out of a job.

Mrs Shin laughs.

SHEN TEH: What can I do for you?

THE UNEMPLOYED MAN: They say you're opening up tomorrow. I thought people sometimes find things in bad condition when they unpack them. Can you spare a fag?

THE WOMAN: What cheek, begging for tobacco. 'Tisn't as if it had been bread.

THE UNEMPLOYED MAN: Bread's expensive. A few puffs at a fag and I'm a new man. I'm so done in.

SHEN TEH *gives him cigarettes*: That's very important, being a new man. I shall open up with you, you'll bring me luck.

The unemployed man hastily lights a cigarette, inhales and goes off coughing.

THE WOMAN: Was that wise, my dear?

MRS SHIN: If that's how you open up you'll be closing down before three days are out.

THE MAN: I bet he had money on him all right.

SHEN TEH: But he said he hadn't anything.

THE NEPHEW: How do you know he wasn't having you on?

SHEN TEH, *worked up*: How do I know he was having me on?

THE WOMAN, *shaking her head*: She can't say no. You're too good, Shen Teh. If you want to hang on to your shop you'd better be able to refuse sometimes.

THE MAN: Say it isn't yours. Say it belongs to a relation and he insists on strict accounts. Why not try it?

MRS SHIN: Anyone would who didn't always want to play Lady Bountiful.

SHEN TEH *laughs*: Grumble away. The room won't be available and the rice goes back in the sack.

THE WOMAN, *shocked*: Is the rice yours too?

SHEN TEH, *to the audience*:

> They are bad.
> They are no man's friend.
> They grudge even a bowl of rice.
> They need it all themselves.
> How can they be blamed?

Enter a little man.

MRS SHIN *sees him and leaves hurriedly*: I'll look in tomorrow then. *Off.*

THE LITTLE MAN *starts after her*: Hey, Mrs Shin! Just the person I want.

THE WOMAN: Does she come regularly? Has she got some claim on you?

SHEN TEH: No claim, but she's hungry: and that's more important.

THE LITTLE MAN: She knows why she's running away. Are you the new proprietress? I see you're stocking up your shelves. But they aren't yours, let me tell you. Unless you pay for them. That old ragamuffin who was squatting here didn't pay. *To the others*: I'm the carpenter, see?

SHEN TEH: But I thought that was part of the fittings I paid for.

THE CARPENTER: Crooks. A pack of crooks. You and this Mrs Shin are thick as thieves. I want my 100 silver dollars, or my name's not Lin To.

SHEN TEH: How can I pay? I've got no money left.

THE CARPENTER: Then I'll have you sold up! On the spot. Pay on the spot or you'll be sold up.

THE MAN *prompts Shen Teh*: Your cousin . . .

SHEN TEH: Can't you make it next month?

THE CARPENTER, *shouting*: No.

SHEN TEH: Don't be too hard, Mr Lin To. I can't satisfy all demands at once. *To the audience*:

> A slight connivance, and one's powers are doubled.
> Look how the cart-horse stops before a tuft of grass:
> Wink one eye for an instant and the horse pulls better.
> Show but a little patience in June and the tree

> By August is sagging with peaches. How
> But for patience could we live together?
> A brief postponement
> Brings the most distant goal within reach.

To the carpenter: Please be patient, just a little, Mr Lin To.

THE CARPENTER: And who is going to be patient with me and my family? *He pulls some of the shelving away from the wall, as if to take it down.* You pay, else I take the shelves with me.

THE WOMAN: My dear Shen Teh, why don't you refer the whole thing to your cousin? *To the carpenter*: Put your claim in writing, and Miss Shen Teh's cousin will pay.

THE CARPENTER: We all know those cousins.

THE NEPHEW: Don't stand there laughing like an idiot. He's a personal friend of mine.

THE MAN: He's sharp as a knife.

THE CARPENTER: All right, he'll get my bill.

He tips the shelving over, sits down on it and writes out his bill.

THE WOMAN: He'll have the clothes off your back for his rotten old planks if you don't stop him. My advice is never admit a claim, right or wrong, or you'll be smothered in claims, right or wrong. Throw a bit of meat in your dustbin, and every mongrel in the place will be at each other's throats in your back yard. What are solicitors for?

SHEN TEH: He has done some work and can't go away with nothing. He has a family too. It's dreadful that I can't pay him. What will the gods say?

THE MAN: You did your bit when you took us in, that's more than enough.

Enter a limping man and a pregnant woman.

THE LIMPING MAN, *to the couple*: So there you are. A credit to the family, I don't think. Going and leaving us waiting at the corner.

THE WOMAN, *embarrassed*: This is my brother Wung and my sister-in-law. *To the two*: Stop nagging and sit quietly out of the way, and don't bother our old friend Miss Shen Teh. *To Shen Teh*: We ought to take them both in, I think, what with my sister-in-law being four months gone. Or are you against it?

SHEN TEH: You are welcome.

THE WOMAN: Thank her. The cups are over there. *To Shen Teh*: They would never have known where to go. Just as well you've got this shop.

SHEN TEH, *laughing to the audience as she brings tea*: Yes, just as well I have got it.

Enter Mrs Mi Tzu, the proprietress, with a document in her hand.

MRS MI TZU: Miss Shen Teh, I am Mrs Mi Tzu, the proprietress of this building. I hope we will get on together. Here is the agreement for the lease. *While Shen Teh studies the agreement*: An auspicious moment, do you not think, gentlemen, when a small business is opened? *She looks round her.* A few gaps on the shelves still, but it will do. I suppose you can provide me with one or two references?

SHEN TEH: Is that necessary?

MRS MI TZU: You see, I have really no idea who you are.

THE MAN: Can we vouch for Miss Shen Teh, maybe? We've known her ever since she first came to town, and we'd cut off our right hands for her.

MRS MI TZU: And who are you?

THE MAN: I am Ma Fu, tobacconist.

MRS MI TZU: Where's your shop?

THE MAN: I haven't got a shop at the moment. It's like this: I've just sold it.

MRS MI TZU: Aha. *To Shen Teh*: And is there no one else who can give me any information about you?

THE WOMAN, *prompting*: Cousin ... your cousin ...

MRS MI TZU: But you must have someone who can tell me what kind of tenant I'm getting in my house. This is a respectable house, my dear. I can't sign any agreement with you otherwise.

SHEN TEH, *slowly, with lowered eyes*: I have got a cousin.

MRS MI TZU: Oh, so you've got a cousin? Round here? We could go straight over now. What is he?

SHEN TEH: He doesn't live here; he's in another town.

THE WOMAN: In Shung, weren't you saying?

SHEN TEH: Mr Shui Ta. In Shung.

THE MAN: But of course I know him. Tall, skinny.

THE NEPHEW, *to the carpenter*: You've had to do with Miss Shen Teh's cousin too, chum. Over the shelving.

THE CARPENTER, *grumpily*: I'm just making out his bill. There you are. *He hands it over.* I'll be back first thing in the morning. *Exit.*

THE NEPHEW, *calling after him, for the proprietress's benefit*: Don't you worry. Her cousin will pay.

MRS MI TZU, *with a keen look at Shen Teh*: Well, I shall also be glad to meet him. Good evening, madam. *Exit.*

THE WOMAN, *after an interval*: It's bound to come out now. You can bet she'll know all about you by the morning.

THE SISTER-IN-LAW, *quietly to the nephew*: This set-up won't last long!

Enter an old man, guided by a boy.

THE BOY, *calling back*: Here they are.

THE WOMAN: Hello, grandpa. *To Shen Teh*: The dear old man. He must have been worrying about us. And the youngster, look how he's grown. He eats like an ostrich. Who else have you got with you?

THE MAN, *looking out*: Only your niece. *To Shen Teh*: A young relation up from the country. I hope we aren't too many for you. We weren't such a big family when you used to live with us, were we? Ah yes, we grew and grew. The worse it got, the more of us there seemed to be. And the more of us there were the worse it got. But we'd better lock up or we'll have no peace.

She shuts the door and all sit down.

THE WOMAN: The great thing is, we mustn't get in your way in the shop. It's up to you to keep the home fires burning. We planned it like this: the kids'll be out during the day, and only grandpa and my sister-in-law will stay, and perhaps me. The others will just be looking in once or twice during the

daytime, see? Light that lamp, boys, and make yourselves
at home.

THE NEPHEW, *facetiously*: I hope that cousin doesn't blow in
tonight, tough old Mr Shui Ta! *The sister-in-law laughs.*

THE BROTHER, *reaching for a cigarette*: One more or less won't
matter.

THE MAN: You bet.

*They all help themselves to something to smoke. The brother hands
round a jug of wine.*

THE NEPHEW: Drinks on old cousin!

THE GRANDFATHER, *solemnly to Shen Teh*: Hullo!

*Shen Teh is confused by this delayed greeting, and bows. In one hand
she holds the carpenter's bill, in the other the agreement for the lease.*

THE WOMAN: Can't you people sing something to entertain our
hostess?

THE NEPHEW: Grandpa can kick off.

They sing:

SONG OF THE SMOKE

THE GRANDFATHER:

Once I believed intelligence would aid me
I was an optimist when I was younger
Now that I'm old I see it hasn't paid me:
How can intelligence compete with hunger?
          And so I said: drop it!
          Like smoke twisting grey
          Into ever colder coldness you'll
          Blow away.

THE MAN:

I saw the conscientious man get nowhere
And so I tried the crooked path instead
But crookedness makes our sort travel slower.
There seems to be no way to get ahead.
          Likewise I say: drop it!
          Like smoke twisting grey
          Into ever colder coldness you'll
          Blow away.

THE NIECE:
>   The old, they say, find little fun in hoping.
>   Time's what they need, and time begins to press.
>   But for the young, they say, the gates are open.
>   They open, so they say, on nothingness.
>>   And I too say: drop it!
>>   Like smoke twisting grey
>>   Into ever colder coldness you'll
>>   Blow away.

THE NEPHEW: Where did that wine come from?

THE SISTER-IN-LAW: He pawned the sack of tobacco.

THE MAN: What? That tobacco was all we had left. We didn't touch it even to get a bed. You dirty bastard!

THE BROTHER: Call me a bastard just because my wife's half frozen? And who's been drinking it? Give me that jug.

They struggle. The shelves collapse.

SHEN TEH *touches them*: O look out for the shop, don't smash everything! It's a gift of the gods. Take whatever's there if you want, but don't smash it!

THE WOMAN, *sceptically*: It's a smaller shop than I thought. A pity we went and told Aunty and the others. If they turn up too there won't be much room.

THE SISTER-IN-LAW: Our hostess is getting a bit frosty too.

There are voices outside, and a knocking on the door.

CRIES: Open up! It's us!

THE WOMAN: Is that you, Aunty? How are we going to manage now?

SHEN TEH: My beautiful shop! Oh, such hopes! No sooner opened, than it is no more. *To the audience*:
>>   The dinghy which might save us
>>   Is straightway sucked into the depths:
>>   Too many of the drowning
>>   Snatch greedily at it.

CRIES *from outside*: Open up!

INTERLUDE
Under a Bridge

The water-seller is crouching by the stream.

WANG, *looking round*: All quiet. That makes four days I have been hiding. They won't find me, I've got my eyes open. I took the same direction as them on purpose. The second day they crossed the bridge; I heard their footsteps overhead. By now they must be a long way off; I have nothing more to fear.

He has leant back and gone to sleep. Music. The slope becomes transparent, and the gods appear.

WANG, *holding his arm in front of his face, as though he were about to be struck*: Don't say anything! I know! I failed to find anybody who would take you into his house! Now I have told you! Now go your way!

THE FIRST GOD: No, you did find somebody. As you left they came up. They took us in for the night; they watched over our sleep; and they lighted our way next morning when we left them. You had told us that she was a good person, and she was good.

WANG: So it was Shen Teh who lodged you?

THE THIRD GOD: Of course.

WANG: And I ran away, I had so little faith! Just because I thought she couldn't come. Because she had been down on her luck she couldn't come.

THE GODS:
O feeble one!
Well-meaning but feeble man!
Where hardship is, he thinks there is no goodness.
Where danger lies, he thinks there is no courage.
O feebleness, that believes no good whatever!
O hasty judgement! O premature despair!

WANG: I am deeply ashamed, Illustrious Ones.

THE FIRST GOD: And now, O water-seller, be so good as to return quickly to the city and look to dear Shen Teh, so that you can keep us posted about her. She is doing well now. She is said to have acquired the money to set up a small shop, so she can freely follow the impulses of her gentle heart. Show some interest in her goodness, for no one can be good for long if goodness is not demanded of him. We for our part wish to travel further and continue our search, and discover still more people like our good person in Szechwan, so that we can put a stop to the rumour which says that the good have found our earth impossible to live on.

They vanish.

2

The Tobacconist's

Sleeping bodies everywhere. The lamp is still burning. A knock.

THE WOMAN *raises herself, drunk with sleep*: Shen Teh! Somebody knocking! Where has the girl got to?

THE NEPHEW: Getting breakfast, I expect. It's on her cousin.

The woman laughs and slouches to the door. Enter a young gentleman, the carpenter behind him.

THE YOUNG GENTLEMAN: I am her cousin.

THE WOMAN, *falling from the clouds*: What did you say you were?

THE YOUNG GENTLEMAN: My name is Shui Ta.

THE FAMILY, *shaking one another awake*: Her cousin! But it was all a joke, she's got no cousin! But here's someone who says he's her cousin! Don't tell me, and at this hour of the day!

THE NEPHEW: If you're our hostess's cousin, mister, get us some breakfast right away, will you?

SHUI TA, *turning out the lamp*: The first customers will be arriving any moment. Please be quick and get dressed so that I can open up my shop.

THE MAN: Your shop? I fancy this shop belongs to our friend Shen Teh? *Shui Ta shakes his head.* What, do you mean to say it's not her shop at all?

THE SISTER-IN-LAW: So she's been having us on. Where's she slunk off to?

SHUI TA: She has been detained. She wishes me to tell you that now I am here she can no longer do anything for you.

THE WOMAN, *shaken*: And we thought she was such a good person.

THE NEPHEW: Don't you believe him! Go and look for her!

THE MAN: Right, we will. *He organises them*: You and you and you and you, go and comb the place for her. Grandpa and us will stay here and hold the fort. The boy can go and find us something to eat. *To the boy*: See that baker's at the corner. Nip over and stuff your shirt full.

THE SISTER-IN-LAW: And don't forget some of those little round cakes.

THE MAN: But mind the baker doesn't catch you. And keep clear of the policeman!

The boy nods and goes off. The others get fully dressed.

SHUI TA: Won't cake-stealing damage the reputation of the shop which has given you refuge?

THE NEPHEW: Don't mind him, we'll soon find her. She'll tell him what's what.

Exeunt nephew, brother, sister-in-law and niece.

THE SISTER-IN-LAW, *as she goes*: Leave us a bit of breakfast.

SHUI TA, *calmly*: You won't find her. My cousin naturally regrets being unable to make unbounded concessions to the laws of hospitality. But I fear you are too numerous. This is a tobacconist's, and it is Miss Shen Teh's livelihood.

THE MAN: Our Shen Teh could never bring herself to say such things.

SHUI TA: You may be right. *To the carpenter*: The unfortunate fact is that the poverty in this city is too much for any individual to correct. Alas, nothing has changed in the eleven centuries since a poet wrote:

That so many of the poor should suffer from cold what can we do to prevent?

To bring warmth to a single body is not much use.
I wish I had a big rug ten thousand feet long,
Which at one time could cover up every inch of the City.*

He starts clearing up the shop.

THE CARPENTER: I see you are trying to straighten out your cousin's affairs. There is a small bill to be settled for the shelves; she has admitted it before witnesses. 100 silver dollars.

SHUI TA, *drawing the bill out of his pocket, not unkindly*: Wouldn't you say that 100 silver dollars was rather much?

THE CARPENTER: No. I can't do it for less. I've a wife and family to look after.

SHUI TA, *hard*: How many children?

THE CARPENTER: Four.

SHUI TA: Then my offer is 20 silver dollars.

THE CARPENTER *laughs*: Are you crazy? These shelves are walnut.

SHUI TA: Then take them away.

THE CARPENTER: What do you mean?

SHUI TA: I can't afford it. I suggest you take your walnut shelves away.

THE WOMAN: One up to you. *She in turn laughs.*

THE CARPENTER, *uncertainly*: I would like Miss Shen Teh to be fetched. She seems to be a decent person, unlike you.

SHUI TA: Obviously. She is ruined.

THE CARPENTER *resolutely seizes some shelving and takes it to the door*: You can stack your goods on the floor then. It doesn't matter to me.

SHUI TA, *to the man*: Give him a hand.

THE MAN *takes some more shelving and takes it to the door with a grin*: Here we go. Chuck the lot out!

THE CARPENTER: You bastard. Do you want my family to starve?

SHUI TA: Let me repeat my offer: you can have 20 silver dollars, to save me stacking my goods on the floor.

* "The Big Rug," from *170 Chinese Poems* by Arthur Waley.

THE CARPENTER: 100.

Shui Ta looks indifferently out of the window. The man sets about removing the shelves.

THE CARPENTER: Anyway, don't smash them into the doorpost, you fool! *In confusion*: But they're made to fit. They won't go anywhere else. The boards had to be cut to size, sir.

SHUI TA: Exactly. That's why I can't offer you more than 20 silver dollars. Because the boards were cut to size.

The woman squeals with delight.

THE CARPENTER *suddenly decides he has had enough*: I can't go on. Keep the shelves and pay me what you like.

SHUI TA: 20 silver dollars.

He lays two big coins on the table. The carpenter takes them.

THE MAN, *bringing back the shelves*: Good enough for a lot of cut-up boards!

THE CARPENTER: About good enough to get drunk on! *Exit.*

THE MAN: Good riddance!

THE WOMAN, *wiping away tears of laughter*: 'But they're walnut!' – 'Take them away!' – '100 silver dollars, I've got four children!' – 'Then I'll pay 20!' – 'But they've been cut to fit!' – 'Exactly, 20 silver dollars!' That's the way to deal with his sort!

SHUI TA: Yes. *Seriously*: Leave here at once.

THE MAN: What, us?

SHUI TA: Yes, you. You are thieves and parasites. Leave at once, waste no time in arguing, and you can still save your skins.

THE MAN: It is better not to take any notice of him. No arguing on an empty stomach. I wonder where the nipper is?

SHUI TA: Yes, where is he? I told you I will not have him here with stolen cakes. *Suddenly shouting*: For the second time. Get out!

They remain seated.

SHUI TA, *calm once more*: All right then.

He walks to the door and bows deeply to someone outside. A police-man looms up in the doorway.

SHUI TA: I take it I am addressing the police representative for this district?

THE POLICEMAN: You are, Mr . . .

SHUI TA: Shui Ta. *They exchange smiles.* Pleasant weather today!

THE POLICEMAN: A trifle warm, perhaps.

SHUI TA: Perhaps a trifle warm.

THE MAN, *softly to his wife*: If he goes on gassing till the kid gets back we'll be done for.

He tries to make Shui Ta a surreptitious sign.

SHUI TA, *without noticing*: It all depends whether one is contemplating the weather from a cool establishment like this or from the dusty street.

THE POLICEMAN: It certainly does.

THE WOMAN: Don't worry. He'll keep away when he sees the copper standing in the door.

SHUI TA: But do come in. It really is cooler here. My cousin and I have opened a shop. Let me tell you that we consider it highly important to be on good terms with the authorities.

THE POLICEMAN *enters*: That is very kind of you, sir. Why yes, it really is cooler in here.

THE MAN, *softly*: He's asked him in just so the kid won't see him.

SHUI TA: Some guests. Distant acquaintances of my cousin's, apparently. They have a journey to make. *Bows are exchanged.* We were just saying goodbye.

THE MAN, *hoarsely*: All right then, we'll be going.

SHUI TA: I will tell my cousin that you thanked her for her hospitality, but could not wait for her return.

Noises from the street and cries of 'Stop thief!'

THE POLICEMAN: What's that about?

The boy appears in the door. Cakes and rolls are tumbling out of his shirt. The woman motions him desperately to get out. He turns and tries to go off.

THE POLICEMAN: You stay here. *He catches hold of him.* Where d'you get those cakes from?

THE BOY: Over there.

THE POLICEMAN: Aha. Stolen, eh?

THE WOMAN: We knew nothing about it. It was the boy's own idea. Little wretch.

THE POLICEMAN: Mr Shui Ta, can you throw any light on this?

Shui Ta remains silent.

THE POLICEMAN: Right. You all come along to the station with me.

SHUI TA: I am exceedingly sorry that anything like this should happen in my shop.

THE WOMAN: He watched the boy go off!

SHUI TA: I can assure you, officer, that I should hardly have invited you in if I had been wanting to conceal a robbery.

THE POLICEMAN: I quite see. You realise I'm only doing my duty, Mr Shui Ta, in taking these persons in custody. *Shui Ta bows.* Get moving, you! *He pushes them out.*

THE GRANDFATHER, *peacefully from the doorway*: Hullo.

Exeunt all except Shui Ta. Enter Mrs Mi Tzu.

MRS MI TZU: So you are the cousin I've heard about? How do the police come to be escorting people away from my building? What does your cousin mean by starting a boarding-house here? That's what comes of taking in people who a moment ago were in cheap digs, begging for crusts from the baker on the corner. I know all about it, you see.

SHUI TA: I do see. People have been speaking against my cousin. They have blamed her for being hungry! She has a bad name for living in poverty. Her reputation is the worst possible: she was down and out!

MRS MI TZU: She was a common or garden . . .

SHUI TA: Pauper; let's say the nasty word aloud.

MRS MI TZU: Oh, don't try and play on my feelings. I am speaking of her way of life, not her income. I have no doubt there was an income from somewhere, or she would hardly have started this shop. No doubt one or two elderly gentlemen looked after that. How does one get hold of a shop? This is a respectable house, sir. The tenants here aren't paying to live under the same roof as that sort of person: no, sir. *Pause.* I am not inhuman, but I have got my obligations.

SHUI TA, *coldly*: Mrs Mi Tzu, I'm a busy man. Just tell me what it will cost to live in this highly respectable house.

MRS MI TZU: Well, you are a cold fish, I'll give you that!

SHUI TA *takes the form of agreement out of the drawer*: It is a very high rent. I take it from this agreement that it is to be paid monthly?

MRS MI TZU, *quickly*: Not for your cousin's sort.

SHUI TA: What does that mean?

MRS MI TZU: That means that people like your cousin have to pay six months' rent in advance: 200 silver dollars.

SHUI TA: 200 silver dollars! That is plain murder! Where am I to find that much? I cannot count on a big turnover here. My one hope is the girls who sew sacks in the cement works, who are supposed to smoke a lot because they find the work so exhausting. But they are badly paid.

MRS MI TZU: You should have thought of that sooner.

SHUI TA: Mrs Mi Tzu, please have a heart! I realise that my cousin made the unforgiveable mistake of giving shelter to some unfortunates. But she will learn. I shall see that she learns. Against that, where could you find a better tenant than one who knows the gutter because he came from there? He'll work his fingers to the bone to pay his rent punctually, he'll do anything, go without anything, sell anything, stick at nothing, and at the same time be as quiet as a mouse, gentle as a fly, submit to you utterly rather than return there. A tenant like that is worth his weight in gold.

MRS MI TZU: 200 silver dollars in advance, or she goes back on the street, where she came from.

Enter the policeman.

THE POLICEMAN: Don't let me disturb you, Mr Shui Ta!

MRS MI TZU: The police really seem remarkably interested in this shop.

THE POLICEMAN: Mrs Mi Tzu, I hope you haven't got a wrong impression. Mr Shui Ta did us a service, and I have come in the name of the police to thank him.

MRS MI TZU: Well, that's no affair of mine. Mr Shui Ta, I trust my proposition will be agreeable to your cousin. I like to be on good terms with my tenants. Good morning, gentlemen.

Exit.

SHUI TA: Good morning, Mrs Mi Tzu.

THE POLICEMAN: Have you been having trouble with Mrs Mi Tzu?

SHUI TA: She is demanding the rent in advance, as she doesn't think my cousin is respectable.

THE POLICEMAN: And can't you raise the money? *Shui Ta remains silent.* But Mr Shui Ta, surely someone like you ought to be able to get credit.

SHUI TA: I dare say. But how is someone like Shen Teh to get credit?

THE POLICEMAN: Are you not staying here then?

SHUI TA: No. And I shall not be able to come again. I could only give her a hand because I was passing through; I just saved her from the worst. Any minute she will be thrown back on her own resources. I am worried as to what will happen.

THE POLICEMAN: Mr Shui Ta, I am sorry to hear that you are having trouble over the rent. I must admit that we began by viewing this shop with mixed feelings, but your decisive action just now showed us the sort of man you are. Speaking for the authorities, we soon find out who we can rely on as a friend of law and order.

SHUI TA, *bitterly*: To save this little shop, officer, which my cousin regards as a gift of the gods, I am prepared to go to the utmost limits of the law. But toughness and duplicity will serve only against one's inferiors, for those limits have been cleverly defined. I am in the position of a man who has just got the rats out of his cellar, when along come the floods. *After a short pause*: Do you smoke?

THE POLICEMAN, *putting two cigars in his pocket*: Our station

would be sorry to see you go, Mr Shui Ta. But you've got to
understand Mrs Mi Tzu's point of view. Shen Teh, let's face
it, lived by selling herself to men. You may ask, what else was
she to do? For instance, how was she to pay her rent? But the
fact remains: it is not respectable. Why not? A: you can't
earn your living by love, or it becomes immoral earnings.
B: respectability means, not with the man who can pay, but
with the man one loves. C: it mustn't be for a handful of rice
but for love. All right, you may say: what's the good of being
so clever over spilt milk? What's she to do? When she has to
find six months' rent? Mr Shui Ta, I must admit I don't
know. *He thinks hard*. Mr Shui Ta, I have got it! All you
need do is to find a husband for her.

Enter a little old woman.

THE OLD WOMAN: I want a good cheap cigar for my husband.
Tomorrow is our fortieth wedding anniversary, you see, and
we are having a little celebration.

SHUI TA, *politely*: Forty years, and still something to celebrate!

THE OLD WOMAN: As far as our means allow! That's our carpet
shop over the way. I hope we are going to be good neighbours,
it's important in these hard times.

SHUI TA *spreads various boxes before her*: Two very familiar
words, I'm afraid.

THE POLICEMAN: Mr Shui Ta, what we need is capital. So I
suggest a marriage.

SHUI TA, *excusing himself to the old woman*: I have been allowing
myself to tell the officer some of my private troubles.

THE POLICEMAN: We've got to find six months' rent. Right, we
marry a bit of money.

SHUI TA: That will not be easy.

THE POLICEMAN: Why not? She's a good match. She owns a
small and promising business. *To the old woman*: What do
you think?

THE OLD WOMAN, *doubtfully*: Well . . .

THE POLICEMAN: An advertisement in the personal column.

THE OLD WOMAN, *reluctant*: If the young lady agrees . . .

THE POLICEMAN: Why shouldn't she agree? I'll draft it out for you. One good turn deserves another. Don't think the authorities have no sympathy for the small and struggling shopkeeper. You play along with us, and in return we draft your matrimonial advertisements! Hahaha!

He hastens to pull out his notebook, licks his pencil stump and starts writing.

SHUI TA, *slowly*: It's not a bad idea.

THE POLICEMAN: 'What respectable gentleman . . . small capital . . . widower considered . . . desires marriage . . . into progressive tobacconist's?' And then we'll add: 'With charming attractive brunette.' How's that?

SHUI TA: You don't feel that's overstating it?

THE OLD WOMAN, *kindly*: Certainly not. I have seen her.

The policeman tears the page out of his notebook and hands it to Shui Ta.

SHUI TA: With horror I begin to realise how much luck one needs to avoid being crushed! What brilliant ideas! What faithful friends! *To the policeman*: Thus for all my decisiveness I was at my wits' end over the rent. And then you came along and helped me with good advice. I really begin to see a way out.

3
Evening in a Public Park

A young man in tattered clothes is watching an aeroplane, which is evidently making a high sweep over the park. He takes a rope from his pocket and looks round him for something. He is making for a big willow-tree, when two prostitutes come up to him. One of them is old, the other is the niece from the family of eight.

THE YOUNG ONE: Evening, young fellow. Coming home with me, dear?

SUN: It could be done, ladies, if you'll stand me a meal.

THE OLD ONE: Are you nuts? *To the young one*: Come on, love. He's just a waste of time. That's that out-of-work pilot.

THE YOUNG ONE: But there won't be a soul in the park now, it's going to rain.

THE OLD ONE: There's always a chance.

They walk on. Sun looks round him, pulls out his rope and throws it over a branch of a willow tree. But he is interrupted again. The two prostitutes return rapidly. They do not see him.

THE YOUNG ONE: It's going to pelt with rain.

Shen Teh is walking up.

THE OLD ONE: Hullo, here she is, the bitch! She got your lot into trouble all right!

THE YOUNG ONE: Not her. It was her cousin. She took us in, and in the end she offered to pay for the cakes. I haven't any bone to pick with her.

THE OLD ONE: I have. *Loudly*: Why, there's our fancy friend with all the money. She's got a shop, but she still wants to pinch our boys off us.

SHEN TEH: Don't jump down my throat! I'm going down to the teahouse by the lake.

THE YOUNG ONE: Is it true you're marrying a widower with three children?

SHEN TEH: Yes, I'm meeting him there.

SUN, *impatiently*: Do your cackling somewhere else, will you? Isn't there anywhere one can get a bit of peace?

THE OLD ONE: Shut up!

Exeunt the two prostitutes.

SUN *calls after them*: Scavengers! *To the audience*: Even in this remote spot they fish tirelessly for victims, even in the thickets, in the rain, they pursue their desperate hunt for custom.

SHEN TEH, *angry*: What call have you got to slang them? *She sees the rope.* Oh!

SUN: What are you gooping at?

SHEN TEH: What's that rope for?

SUN: Move on, sister, move on! I've got no money, nothing, not a copper. And if I had I'd buy a drink of water, not you.

It starts raining.

SHEN TEH: What's that rope for? You're not to do it!
SUN: Mind your own business! And get out of the way!
SHEN TEH: It's raining.
SUN: Don't you try sheltering under my tree.
SHEN TEH *remains motionless in the rain*: No.
SUN: Why not give up, sister, it's no use. You can't do business with me. Besides, you're too ugly, Bandy legs.
SHEN TEH: That's not true.
SUN: I don't want to see them! All right, come under the bloody tree, since it's raining!

She approaches slowly and sits down under the tree.

SHEN TEH: Why do you want to do that?
SUN: Would you like to know? Then I'll tell you, so as to be rid of you. *Pause.* Do you know what an airman is?
SHEN TEH: Yes, I once saw some airmen in a teahouse.
SUN: Oh no you didn't. One or two windy idiots in flying helmets, I expect: the sort who's got no ear for his engine and no feeling for his machine. Gets into a kite by bribing the hangar superintendent. Tell a type like that: now stall your crate at 2,000, down through the clouds, then catch her up with the flick of the stick, and he'll say: But that's not in the book. If you can't land your kite gently as lowering your bottom you're not an airman, you're an idiot. Me, I'm an airman. And yet I'm the biggest idiot of the lot, because I read all the manuals in flying school at Pekin. But just one page of one manual I happened to miss, the one where it says Airmen Not Wanted. And so I became an airman without an aircraft, a mail pilot without mail. What that means you wouldn't understand.
SHEN TEH: I think I do understand all the same.
SUN: No, I'm telling you you can't understand. And that means you can't understand.

SHEN TEH, *half laughing, half crying*: When we were children we had a crane with a broken wing. He was very tame and didn't mind our teasing him, and used to come strutting after us and scream if we went too fast for him. But in the autumn and the spring, when the great flocks of birds flew over our village, he became very restless, and I could understand why.

SUN: Stop crying.

SHEN TEH: Yes.

SUN: It's bad for the complexion.

SHEN TEH: I'm stopping.

She dries her tears on her sleeve. Leaning against the tree, but without turning towards her, he reaches for her face.

SUN: You don't even know how to wipe your face properly.

He wipes it for her with a handkerchief.

SUN: If you've got to sit there and stop me from hanging myself you might at least say something.

SHEN TEH: I don't know what.

SUN: Why do you want to hack me down, sister, as a matter of interest?

SHEN TEH: It frightens me. I'm sure you only felt like that because the evening's so dreary. *To the audience*:
> In our country
> There should be no dreary evenings
> Or tall bridges over rivers
> Even the hour between night and morning
> And the whole winter season too, that is dangerous.
> For in face of misery
> Only a little is needed
> Before men start throwing
> Their unbearable life away.

SUN: Tell me about yourself.

SHEN TEH: What is there? I've got a small shop.

SUN, *ironically*: Oh, so you haven't got a flat, you've got a shop!

SHEN TEH, *firmly*: I've got a shop, but before that I was on the streets.

SUN: And the shop, I take it, was a gift of the gods?

SHEN TEH: Yes.

SUN: One fine evening they stood before you and said: Here's some money for you.

SHEN TEH, *laughing quietly*: One morning.

SUN: You're not exactly entertaining.

SHEN TEH, *after a pause*: I can play the zither a bit, and do imitations. *In a deep voice she imitates a dignified gentleman*: 'How idiotic, I must have come without my wallet!' But then I got the shop. The first thing I did was give away my zither. From now on, I told myself, you can be a complete jellyfish and it won't matter.

> How rich I am, I told myself.
> I walk alone. I sleep alone.
> For one whole year, I told myself
> I'll have no dealings with a man.

SUN: But now you're going to marry one? The one in the tea-house by the lake.

Shen Teh says nothing.

SUN: As a matter of interest, what do you know of love?

SHEN TEH: Everything.

SUN: Nothing, sister. Or was it perhaps pleasant?

SHEN TEH: No.

Sun strokes her face, without turning towards her.

SUN: Is that pleasant?

SHEN TEH: Yes.

SUN: Easily satisfied, you are. God, what a town.

SHEN TEH: Haven't you got friends?

SUN: A whole lot, but none that like hearing that I'm still out of a job. They make a face as if someone were complaining that the sea's wet. Have you got a friend, if it comes to that?

SHEN TEH, *hesitantly*: A cousin.

SUN: Then don't you trust him an inch.

SHEN TEH: He was only here once. Now he has gone off and is never coming back. But why do you talk as if you'd given up hope? They say: to give up hope, is to give up kindness.

SUN: Just talk on! At least it's something to hear a human voice.

SHEN TEH, *eagerly*: There are still friendly people, for all our wretchedness. When I was little once I was carrying a bundle of sticks and fell. An old man helped me up and even gave me a penny. I have often thought of it. Those who have least to eat give most gladly. I suppose people just like showing what they are good at; and how can they do it better than by being friendly? Crossness is just a way of being inefficient. Whenever someone is singing a song or building a machine or planting rice it is really friendliness. You are friendly too.

SUN: It doesn't seem hard by your definition.

SHEN TEH: And that was a raindrop.

SUN: Where?

SHEN TEH: Between my eyes.

SUN: More to the left or more to the right?

SHEN TEH: More to the left.

SUN: Good. *After a moment, sleepily*: So you're through with men?

SHEN TEH, *smiling*: But my legs aren't bandy.

SUN: Perhaps not.

SHEN TEH: Definitely not.

SUN, *wearily leaning back against the tree*: But as I haven't eaten for two days or drunk for one, I couldn't love you, sister, even if I wanted.

SHEN TEH: It is good in the rain.

Wang, the water-seller appears. He sings.

WANG:

THE WATER-SELLER'S SONG IN THE RAIN

> I sell water. Who will taste it?
> – Who would want to in this weather?
> All my labour has been wasted
> Fetching these few pints together.
> I stand shouting Buy my Water!
> And nobody thinks it
> Worth stopping and buying
> Or greedily drinks it.

(Buy water, you devils!)

> O to stop the leaky heaven
> Hoard what stock I've got remaining:
> Recently I dreamt that seven
> Years went by without it raining.
> How they'd all shout Give me Water!
> How they'd fight for my good graces
> And I'd make their further treatment
> Go by how I liked their faces.

(Stay thirsty, you devils!)

> Wretched weeds, you're through with thirsting
> Heaven must have heard you praying.
> You can drink until you're bursting
> Never bother about paying.
> I'm left shouting Buy my Water!
> And nobody thinks it
> Worth stopping and buying
> Or greedily drinks it.

(Buy water, you devils!)

The rain has stopped. Shen Teh sees Wang and runs towards him.

SHEN TEH: Oh Wang, so you have come back. I have looked after your pole for you.

WANG: Thank you for taking care of it! How are you, Shen Teh?

SHEN TEH: Well. I have got to know a very brave and clever person. And I should like to buy a cup of your water.

WANG: Throw your head back and open your mouth, and you can have as much water as you want. The willow tree is still dripping.

SHEN TEH: But I want your water, Wang.

> Laboriously carried
> Exhausting to its bearer
> And hard to sell, because it is raining.
> And I need it for the man over yonder.
> He is an airman. An airman
> Is braver than other humans. With the clouds for
> companions

Daring enormous tempests
He flies through the heavens and brings
To friends in far countries
The friendly post.

She pays and runs over to Sun with the cup.

SHEN TEH *calls back to Wang, laughing*: He has fallen asleep.
Hopelessness and the rain and I have tired him out.

INTERLUDE

Wang's sleeping-place under a Culvert

*The water-seller is asleep. Music. The culvert becomes transparent,
and the gods appear to him as he dreams.*

WANG, *beaming*: I have seen her, O Illustrious Ones! She has
not changed.

THE FIRST GOD: That gives us pleasure.

WANG: She is in love! She showed me her friend. Truly things
are going well for her.

THE FIRST GOD: That is good to hear. Let us hope that she will
be strengthened in her pursuit of goodness.

WANG: Indeed yes! She is performing all the charitable deeds
she can.

THE FIRST GOD: Charitable deeds? What sort? Tell us about
them, dear Wang.

WANG: She has a friendly word for everyone.

THE FIRST GOD, *keenly*: What else?

WANG: It is rare that a man is allowed to leave her shop without
something to smoke, just for lack of money.

THE FIRST GOD: That sounds satisfactory. Any more?

WANG: She has taken in a family of eight.

THE FIRST GOD, *triumphantly to the second*: Eight, indeed! *To
Wang*: Have you anything else you can tell us?

WANG: Although it was raining she bought a cup of water from
me.

THE FIRST GOD: Yes, minor charities of that sort. Of course.

WANG: But they eat into the money. A small business doesn't make all that much.

THE FIRST GOD: True, true! But a prudent gardener can work wonders with his little patch.

WANG: That is just what she does! Every morning she distributes rice; believe me, it must cost more than half her earnings!

THE FIRST GOD, *slightly disappointed*: I am not denying it. I am not displeased with her start.

WANG: Remember, times are not easy! She had to call in a cousin once, as her shop was getting into difficulties.

> Hardly was a shelter erected against the wind
> Than the ruffled birds of the whole wintry heaven
> Came tumbling flying and
> Squabbled for a place and the hungry fox gnawed through
> The flimsy wall and the one-legged wolf
> Knocked the little rice-bowl over.

In other words the business was too much for her to manage. But everyone agrees that she is a good girl. They have begun to call her 'The Angel of the Slums'. So much good goes out from her shop. Whatever Lin To the carpenter may say!

THE FIRST GOD: What's that? Does Lin To the carpenter speak ill of her?

WANG: Oh, he only says the shelving in the shop wasn't quite paid for.

THE SECOND GOD: What are you telling us? A carpenter not paid? In Shen Teh's shop? How could she permit that?

WANG: I suppose she didn't have the money.

THE SECOND GOD: No matter: one pays one's debts. One cannot afford even the appearance of irregularity. The letter of the law has first to be fulfilled; then its spirit.

WANG: But Illustrious Ones, it was only her cousin, not herself.

THE SECOND GOD: Then that cousin must never again enter her door.

WANG, *dejected*: I have understood, Illustrious One! But in Shen Teh's defence let me just say that her cousin is supposed to be a most reputable business man. Even the police respect him.

THE FIRST GOD: This cousin will not be condemned without a hearing either. I know nothing of business, I admit; perhaps we ought to find out what is thought usual in such matters. But business indeed! Is it so very necessary? Nowadays there is nothing but business. Were the Seven Good Kings in business? Did Kung the Just sell fish? What has business to do with an upright and honourable life?

THE SECOND GOD, *with a bad cold*: In any case it must not be allowed to occur again.

He turns to leave. The other two gods likewise turn.

THE THIRD GOD, *the last to leave, embarrassedly*: Forgive our rather sharp tone today! We are very tired, and we have slept too little. Oh, those nights! The well-off give us the best possible recommendations to the poor, but the poor have too few rooms.

THE GODS *grumble as they move off*: Broken reeds, even the best of them! Nothing conclusive! Pitiful, pitiful! All from the heart, of course, but it adds up to nothing! At least she ought to . . .

They can no longer be heard.

WANG *calls after them*: Do not be too hard on us, O Illustrious Ones! Do not ask for everything at once!

4

Square in front of Shen Teh's Shop

A barber's, a carpet shop and Shen Teh's tobacconist's shop. It is Monday. Outside Shen Teh's shop wait two survivors of the family of eight – the grandfather and the sister-in-law. Also the unemployed man and Mrs Shin.

THE SISTER-IN-LAW: She never came home last night!

MRS SHIN: Astonishing behaviour! We manage to get rid of this maniac of a cousin and there's nothing to stop her having a little rice to spare now and again, when off she goes for the night chasing around God knows where!

Loud voices are heard from the barber's. Wang staggers out followed by Mr Shu Fu, the stout barber, with a heavy pair of curling tongs in his hand.

MR SHU FU: I'll teach you to come bothering my customers with your stinking water! Take your mug and get out!

Wang reaches for the mug which Mr Shu Fu is holding out to him, and gets a blow on the hand with the curling tongs, so that he screams.

MR SHU FU: Take that! Let that be a lesson to you.

He puffs back to his shop.

THE UNEMPLOYED MAN *picks up the mug and hands it to Wang:* You can have him up for hitting you.

WANG: My hand's gone.

THE UNEMPLOYED MAN: Any bones broken?

WANG: I can't move it.

THE UNEMPLOYED MAN: Sit down and bathe it a bit.

MRS SHIN: The water won't cost you much, anyway.

THE SISTER-IN-LAW: Eight o'clock already, and one can't even lay hands on a bit of rag here. She has to go gallivanting off! A disgrace!

MRS SHIN, *darkly:* She's forgotten us, that's what!

Shen Teh comes down the street carrying a pot of rice.

SHEN TEH, *to the audience*: I had never seen the city at dawn. These were the hours when I used to lie with my filthy blanket over my head, terrified to wake up. Today I mixed with the newsboys, with the men who were washing down the streets, with the ox-carts bringing fresh vegetables in from the fields. It was a long walk from Sun's neighbourhood to here, but with every step I grew happier. I had always been told that when one is in love one walks on air, but the wonderful thing is that one walks on earth, on tarmac. I tell you, at dawn the blocks of buildings are like rubbish heaps with little lights glowing in them; the sky is pink but still transparent, clear of dust. I tell you, you miss a great deal if you are not in love and cannot see your city at that hour when she rises from her couch like a sober old craftsman, filling his lungs with fresh air and reaching for his tools, as the poets have it. *To the group waiting*: Good morning! Here is your rice! *She shares it out, then notices Wang*: Good morning, Wang. I am light-headed today. All along the way I looked at my reflection in the shop windows, and now I would like to buy myself a shawl. *After a short hesitation*: I should so like to look beautiful.

She turns quickly into the carpet shop.

MR SHU FU, *who is again standing in his doorway, to the audience*: I am smitten today with the beauty of Miss Shen Teh, the owner of the tobacconist's opposite, whom I have never previously noticed. I have watched her for three minutes, and I believe I am already in love. An infinitely charming person! *To Wang*: Get to hell, you lout!

He turns back into the barber's shop. Shen Teh and an extremely old couple, the carpet-dealer and his wife, come out of the carpet-shop. Shen Teh is carrying a shawl, the carpet-dealer a mirror.

THE OLD WOMAN: It's very pretty and not at all dear; there's a small hole at the bottom.

SHEN TEH, *trying the shawl on the old woman's arm*: I like the green one too.

THE OLD WOMAN, *smiling*: But I'm afraid it's in perfect condition.

SHEN TEH: Yes, a pity. I cannot undertake too much with my shop. The income is small, and there are many expenses.

THE OLD WOMAN: For charity; don't you do so much. When you are starting every bowl of rice counts, eh?

SHEN TEH *tries on the shawl with the hole in it*: Except that I have to; only at present I'm light-headed. Do you think the colour suits me?

THE OLD WOMAN: You had better ask a man that question.

SHEN TEH *calls to the old man*: Does it suit me?

THE OLD MAN: Why don't you ask . . .

SHEN TEH, *very politely*: No, I am asking you.

THE OLD MAN, *equally politely*: The shawl suits you. But wear it dull side out.

Shen Teh pays.

THE OLD WOMAN: If you don't like it I will always change it for another. *Draws her aside*: Has he any money?

SHEN TEH, *laughing*: O goodness no.

THE OLD WOMAN: Will you be able to pay your half-year's rent?

SHEN TEH: The rent! It had clean gone out of my mind!

THE OLD WOMAN: I thought it had! And Monday will be the first of the month. I have something to suggest. You know: my husband and I were a little doubtful about the marriage advertisement once we had got to know you. We decided we'd help you out if need be. We've put something by, and we can lend you the 200 silver dollars. If you like you can make over your stock to us as security. But of course we don't need anything in writing.

SHEN TEH: Would you really lend money to such a scatter-brained person?

THE OLD WOMAN: To be honest, we'd think twice about lending it to your cousin, who is definitely not scatter-brained, but we'd gladly lend it to you.

THE OLD MAN *comes up*: All fixed?

SHEN TEH: I wish the gods could have heard your wife just

then, Mr Deng. They are looking for good and happy people. And I'm sure you must be happy, to be helping me out of the troubles that love has brought me.

The two old people smile at one another.

THE OLD MAN: Here is the money.

He hands her an envelope. Shen Teh accepts it and bows. The old people bow too. They go back to their shop.

SHEN TEH, *to Wang, holding up the envelope*: This is six months' rent. Isn't that a miracle? And Wang, what do you think of my new shawl?

WANG: Did you buy it for the man I saw in the park?

Shen Teh nods.

MRS SHIN: You might choose to look at his hand instead of retailing your shady adventures!

SHEN TEH, *alarmed*: What's the matter with your hand?

MRS SHIN: The barber smashed it with his curling tongs in front of our eyes.

SHEN TEH, *horrified at her heedlessness*: And I didn't notice! You must go to the doctor at once, or your hand will go stiff and you'll never be able to work properly again. It's a frightful disaster. Come on, get up! Hurry!

THE UNEMPLOYED MAN: He doesn't want the doctor; he wants the magistrate! The barber's a rich man, and he ought to get compensation.

WANG: Do you think there's a chance?

MRS SHIN: If you really can't use it. Can you?

WANG: I don't think so. It's already very swollen. Would it mean a pension for life?

MRS SHIN: You need a witness, of course.

WANG: But you all saw! You can all of you bear me out.

He looks round. Unemployed man, grandfather, sister-in-law: all are sitting against the wall and eating. No one looks up.

SHEN TEH, *to Mrs Shin*: You yourself saw it, didn't you?

MRS SHIN: I don't want to get mixed up with the police.

SHEN TEH, *to the sister-in-law*: What about you then?

THE SISTER-IN-LAW: Me? I wasn't looking!

MRS SHIN: Of course you were looking. I saw you looking!
You're just scared because the barber's got too much pull.

SHEN TEH, *to the grandfather*: I am sure that you will confirm
what happened.

THE SISTER-IN-LAW: They wouldn't listen to him. He's gaga.

SHEN TEH, *to the unemployed man*: It may mean a pension for
life.

THE UNEMPLOYED MAN: They've taken my name twice for begging. It won't do him much good if I give evidence.

SHEN TEH, *incredulous*: Do you mean to say that not one of you
will say what happened? His hand gets broken in full day-
light, in front of you all, and not one will open his mouth.
Angrily:

O you unfortunates!

Your brother is mishandled before you, and you just shut
your eyes.

Injured, he screams aloud, and you keep mum.

The bully swaggers round, picks out his victim

And you say: he'll spare us, for we hide our displeasure.

What sort of a town is that, what sort of humans are you?

When an injustice takes place in a town there must be an
uproar

And where there is no uproar it is better the town disappears

In flames before the night falls.

Wang, if nobody who saw it will be your witness, then I will
be your witness and say that I saw it.

MRS SHIN: It'll be perjury.

WANG: I don't know if I can allow that. But perhaps I have to
allow it. *Looking anxiously at his hand*: Do you think it has
swollen enough? It looks to me as if it has started to go down?

THE UNEMPLOYED MAN, *calming him*: No, it certainly hasn't
gone down.

WANG: Are you sure? Ah yes, I do believe it's swelling a bit

more. Possibly my wrist is broken! I'd better go straight to
the magistrate.

*Holding his hand carefully and still looking at it, he hurries off.
Mrs Shin enters the barber's shop.*

THE UNEMPLOYED MAN: She's gone to the barber's to butter
him up.

THE SISTER-IN-LAW: It's not for us to change the world.

SHEN TEH, *discouraged*: I didn't mean to be rude to you. It's
just that I was shocked. No, I did mean to be rude to you.
Get out of my sight!

*The unemployed man, the sister-in-law and the grandfather go off
eating and grumbling.*

SHEN TEH, *to the audience*:
        They cannot respond. Where they are stationed
        They stay put, and when turned away
        They quickly yield place!
        Nothing now moves them. Only
        The smell of cooking will make them look up.

An old woman comes hurrying up. It is Sun's mother, Mrs Yang.

MRS YANG, *out of breath*: Are you Miss Shen Teh? My son has
told me everything. I am Sun's mother, Mrs Yang. Think
of it, he has got the chance of a job as a pilot! He got a letter
from Pekin this morning, just now. From one of the superin-
tendents in the postal service.

SHEN TEH: That means he can fly again? Oh, Mrs Yang!

MRS YANG: But it will cost a lot: 500 silver dollars.

SHEN TEH: That's a great deal, but money must not stand in
his way. After all, I've got the shop.

MRS YANG: If you could only do something!

SHEN TEH *embraces her*: If I could help him!

MRS YANG: You would be giving a chance to a very gifted
individual!

SHEN TEH: Why should they stop a man from applying his gifts?
After a pause: Except that I shall not get enough for the shop,

and the 200 silver dollars which I have got in cash are only a loan. Of course you can have those now. I will sell my stock and pay them back out of that.

She gives her the old couple's money.

MRS YANG: O Miss Shen Teh, a friend in need is a friend indeed. And they were all calling him the dead pilot, because they said he has as much chance of flying again as a corpse.

SHEN TEH: We still need 300 silver dollars for the job, though. Mrs Yang, we must think. *Slowly*: I know someone who might perhaps help. Someone who has advised me before. I didn't really want to have to resort to him again; he is too smart and too tough. This will definitely be the last time. But a pilot has got to fly, that is obvious.

Sound of engines in the distance.

MRS YANG: If your friend could only raise the money! Look, there goes the morning mail service to Pekin!

SHEN TEH, *with determination*: Wave to it, Mrs Yang. I'm sure the pilot can see us! *She waves her shawl.* Go on, wave!

MRS YANG, *waving*: Do you know the pilot?

SHEN TEH: No. I know a pilot. For the man without hope shall fly, Mrs Yang. One of us at least shall be able to fly above all this wretchedness; one at least shall rise above us all!

To the audience:

Yang Sun, my loved one, with the clouds for companions!
Daring enormous tempests
Flying through the heavens and bringing
To friends in far countries
The friendly post.

INTERLUDE
in front of the curtain

Shen Teh enters, carrying Shui Ta's mask and costume, and sings the

SONG OF THE DEFENCELESSNESS OF THE GOOD AND THE GODS

SHEN TEH:

In our country
The capable man needs luck. Only
If he has mighty backers
Can he prove his capacity.
The good
Have no means of helping themselves and the gods are
   powerless.
    So why can't the gods launch a great operation
    With bombers and battleships, tanks and destroyers
    And rescue the good by a ruthless invasion?
    Then maybe the wicked would cease to annoy us.

She puts on Shui Ta's costume and takes a few steps in his way of walking.

The good
Cannot remain good for long in our country
Where cupboards are bare, housewives start to squabble.
Oh, the divine commandments
Are not much use against hunger.
    So why can't the gods share out what they've created
    Come down and distribute the bounties of nature
    And allow us, once hunger and thirst have been sated
    To mix with each other in friendship and pleasure?

She dons Shui Ta's mask and sings on in his voice.

In order to win one's mid-day meal
One needs the toughness which elsewhere builds empires.
Except twelve others be trampled down
The unfortunate cannot be helped.

So why can't the gods make a simple decision
That goodness must conquer in spite of its weakness? –
Then back up the good with an armoured division
Command it to: 'fire!' and not tolerate meekness?

5

The Tobacconist's

Shui Ta sits behind the counter and reads the paper. He takes no notice of Mrs Shin, who is cleaning the place and talking.

MRS SHIN: A small business like this soon goes downhill, believe me, once certain rumours get around locally. This shady affair between the young lady and that fellow Yang Sun from the Yellow Alley, it was high time a proper gentleman like you came and cleared it up. Don't forget that Mr Shu Fu, the hairdresser next door, a gentleman who owns twelve houses and has only one wife, and an old one at that, hinted to me yesterday that he took a rather flattering interest in the young lady. He went so far as to ask about her financial standing. I'd say that showed real partiality.

Getting no answer, she finally leaves with her bucket.

SUN'S VOICE, *from outside*: Is this Miss Shen Teh's shop?
MRS SHIN'S VOICE: Yes. But her cousin's there today.

Shui Ta runs to a mirror, with Shen Teh's light steps, and is just beginning to arrange his hair when he realises his mistake. He turns away with a soft laugh. Enter Yang Sun. Behind him appears the inquisitive Mrs Shin. She goes past him into the back of the shop.

SUN: I am Yang Sun. *Shui Ta bows.* Is Shen Teh in?
SHUI TA: No, she is not in.
SUN: But I expect you're in the picture about me and her? *He begins to take stock of the shop.* A real shop, large as life. I always thought she was putting it on a bit. *He examines the boxes and china pots with satisfaction.* Oh boy, I'm going to be flying again. *He helps himself to a cigar, and Shui Ta gives*

him a light. Do you think we can squeeze another 300 dollars out of the business?

SHUI TA: May I ask: is it your intention to proceed to an immediate sale?

SUN: Why? Have we got the 300 in cash? *Shui Ta shakes his head.* It was good of her to produce the 200 at once. But I've got to have the other 300 or I'm stuck.

SHUI TA: Perhaps she was a bit hasty in offering you the money. It may cost her her business. They say, haste is the wind that blew the house down.

SUN: I need it now or not at all. And the girl's not one to hesitate when it's a question of giving. Between ourselves, she hasn't hesitated much so far.

SHUI TA: Really?

SUN: All to her credit, of course.

SHUI TA: May I ask how the 500 dollars will be used?

SUN: Why not? As you seem to be checking up on me. The airport superintendent in Pekin is a friend of mine from flying school, and he can get me the job if I cough up 500 silver dollars.

SHUI TA: Isn't that an unusually large sum?

SUN: No. He has got to prove negligence against a highly conscientious pilot with a large family. You get me? That's between us, by the way, and there's no need for Shen Teh to know.

SHUI TA: Perhaps not. One point though: won't the superintendent be selling you up the river a month later?

SUN: Not me. No negligence with me. I've been long enough without a job.

SHUI TA *nods*: It is the hungry dog who pulls the cart home quickest. *He studies him for a moment or two*: That's a very big responsibility. You are asking my cousin, Mr Yang Sun, to give up her small property and all her friends in this town, and to place herself entirely in your hands. I take it your intention is to marry Shen Teh?

SUN: I'd be prepared to.

SHUI TA: Then wouldn't it be a pity to let the business go for a few silver dollars? You won't get much for a quick sale. The 200 silver dollars that you've already got would guarantee the rent for six months. Do you not feel at all tempted to carry on the tobacconist's business?

SUN: What, me? Have people see Yang Sun the pilot serving behind a counter? 'Good morning, sir; do you prefer Turkish or Virginia?' That's no career for Yang Suns, not in the twentieth century!

SHUI TA: And is flying a career, may I ask?

SUN *takes a letter from his pocket*: They're paying me 250 silver dollars a month, sir. Here is the letter; see for yourself. Look at the stamp, postmarked Pekin.

SHUI TA: 250 silver dollars? That is a lot.

SUN: Do you think I'd fly for nothing?

SHUI TA: It sounds like a good job. Mr Yang Sun, my cousin has asked me to help you get this pilot's job which means so much to you. Looking at it from her point of view I see no insuperable objection to her following the bidding of her heart. She is fully entitled to share in the delights of love. I am prepared to realise everything here. Here comes Mrs Mi Tzu, the landlady; I will ask her advice about the sale.

MRS MI TZU *enters*: Good morning, Mr Shui Ta. I suppose it's about your rent that's due the day after tomorrow?

SHUI TA: Mrs Mi Tzu, circumstances have arisen which make it doubtful whether my cousin will carry on with the business. She is contemplating marriage, and her future husband – *he introduces Yang Sun* – Mr Yang Sun, is taking her to Pekin where they wish to start a new life. If I can get a good price for my tobacco I shall sell it.

MRS MI TZU: How much do you need?

SUN: 300 in cash.

SHUI TA, *quickly*: No, no. 500!

MRS MI TZU, *to Sun*: Perhaps I can help you out. How much did your stock cost?

SHUI TA: My cousin originally paid 1000 silver dollars, and very little of it has been sold.

MRS MI TZU: 1000 silver dollars! She was swindled, of course.

I'll make you an offer: you can have 300 silver dollars for the whole business, if you move out the day after tomorrow.

SUN: All right. That's it, old boy!

SHUI TA: It's too little!

SUN: It's enough!

SHUI TA: I must have at least 500.

SUN: What for?

SHUI TA: May I just discuss something with my cousin's fiancé? *Aside to Sun*: All this stock of tobacco is pledged to two old people against the 200 silver dollars which you got yesterday.

SUN, *slowly*: Is there anything about it in writing?

SHUI TA: No.

SUN, *to Mrs Mi Tzu after a short pause*: 300 will do us.

MRS MI TZU: But I have to be sure that the business has no outstanding debts.

SUN: You answer.

SHUI TA: The business has no outstanding debts.

SUN: How soon can we have the 300?

MRS MI TZU: The day after tomorrow, and you had better think it over. Put the sale off for a month and you will get more. I can offer you 300, and that's only because I'm glad to help where it seems to be a case of young love. *Exit*.

SUN, *calling after her*: It's a deal! Lock, stock and barrel for 300, and our troubles are over. *To Shui Ta*: I suppose we might get a better offer in the next two days? Then we could even pay back the 200.

SHUI TA: Not in the time. We shan't get a single dollar over Mrs Mi Tzu's 300. Have you got the money for both your tickets, and enough to tide you over?

SUN: Sure.

SHUI TA: How much?

SUN: Anyway, I'll raise it even if I have to steal it!

SHUI TA: Oh, so that's another sum that has to be raised?

SUN: Don't worry, old boy. I'll get to Pekin all right.

SHUI TA: It costs quite a bit for two.

SUN: Two? I'm leaving the girl here. She'd only be a liability at first.

SHUI TA: I see.

SUN: Why do you look at me as if I was something the cat had brought in? Beggars can't be choosers.

SHUI TA: And what is my cousin to live on?

SUN: Can't you do something for her?

SHUI TA: I will look into it. *Pause.* I should like you to hand me back the 200 silver dollars, Mr Yang Sun, and leave them with me until you are in a position to show me two tickets to Pekin.

SUN: My dear cousin, I should like you to mind your own business.

SHUI TA: Miss Shen Teh . . .

SUN: You just leave her to me.

SHUI TA: . . . may not wish to proceed with the sale of her business when she hears . . .

SUN: O yes she will.

SHUI TA: And you are not afraid of what I may have to say against it?

SUN: My dear man!

SHUI TA: You seem to forget that she is flesh and blood, and has a mind of her own.

SUN, *amused*: It astounds me what people imagine about their female relations and the effect of sensible argument. Haven't they ever told you about the power of love, the twitching of the flesh? You want to appeal to her reason? She hasn't any reason! All she's had is a life-time of ill-treatment, poor thing! If I put my hand on her shoulder and say 'You're coming with me,' she'll hear bells and not recognise her own mother.

SHUI TA, *laboriously*: Mr Yang Sun!

SUN: Mr . . . whatever your name is!

SHUI TA: My cousin is indebted to you because . . .

SUN: Let's say because I've got my hand inside her blouse? Stuff that in your pipe and smoke it! *He takes another cigar, then sticks a few in his pocket, and finally puts the box under his arm.* You're not to go to her empty-handed: we're getting married, and that's settled. And she'll bring the 300 with her or else you will: either her or you. *Exit*.

MRS SHIN *sticks her head out of the back room*: How very dis-
agreeable! And the whole Yellow Alley knows that he's got
the girl exactly where he wants her.

SHUI TA, *crying out*: The business has gone! He's not in love.
This means ruin. I am lost! *He begins to rush round like a
captive animal, continually repeating, 'The business has gone!'
– until he suddenly stops and addresses Mrs Shin*: Mrs Shin,
you grew up in the gutter and so did I. Are we irresponsible?
No. Do we lack the necessary brutality? No. I am ready to
take you by the scruff of the neck and shake you until you
spit out the farthing you stole from me, and you know it.
Times are frightful, the town is hell, but we scrabble up the
naked walls. Then one of us is overcome by disaster: he is in
love. That is enough, he is lost. A single weakness, and you
can be shovelled away. How can one remain free of every
weakness, above all of the most deadly, of love? It is intoler-
able! It costs too much! Tell me, has one got to spend one's
whole life on the look-out? What sort of world do we live in?

Love's caresses merge in strangulation.
Love's sighs grow into a scream of fear.
What are the vultures hovering for?
A girl is keeping an appointment.

MRS SHIN: I think I had better fetch the barber. You must talk
to the barber. He is a man of honour. The barber: that's the
right man for your cousin.

*Getting no answer, she hurries away. Shui Ta continues rushing
around until Mr Shu Fu enters, followed by Mrs Shin, who however is forced to withdraw at a gesture from Mr Shu Fu.*

SHUI TA *turns to him*: My dear sir, rumour has it that you have
shown a certain interest in my cousin. You must allow me to
set aside the laws of propriety, which call for a measure of
reserve, for the young lady is at the moment in great danger.

MR SHU FU: Oh!

SHUI TA: Proprietress of her own business until a few hours ago, my cousin is now little more than a beggar. Mr Shu Fu, this shop is bankrupt.

MR SHU FU: Mr Shui Ta, Miss Shen Teh's attraction lies less in the soundness of her business than in the goodness of her heart. You can tell a lot from the name they give the young lady round here: The Angel of the Slums!

SHUI TA: My dear sir, this goodness has cost my cousin 200 silver dollars in a single day! There are limits.

MR SHU FU: Allow me to put forward a different opinion: is it not time that all limits to this goodness were removed? It is the young lady's nature to do good. What is the sense of her feeding four people, as she so moves me by doing every morning! Why should she not feed four hundred? I hear for instance that she is desperate to find shelter for a few homeless. My buildings across the cattleyard are unoccupied. They are at her disposal. And so on and so forth. Mr Shui Ta, have I the right to hope that such thoughts as these which I have lately been entertaining may find a willing listener in Miss Shen Teh?

SHUI TA: Mr Shu Fu, she will listen with admiration to such lofty thoughts.

Enter Wang with the policeman. Mr Shu Fu turns round and examines the shelves.

WANG: Is Miss Shen Teh here?

SHUI TA: No.

WANG: I am Wang, the water-seller. I suppose you are Mr Shui Ta?

SHUI TA: Quite correct. Good morning, Wang.

WANG: I am a friend of Shen Teh's.

SHUI TA: I know that you are one of her oldest friends.

WANG, *to the policeman*: See? *To Shui Ta*: I have come about my hand.

THE POLICEMAN: He can't use it, there's no denying.

SHUI TA, *quickly*: I see you want a sling for your arm. *He fetches a shawl from the back room and tosses it to Wang.*

WANG: But that's her new shawl.

SHUI TA: She won't need it.

WANG: But she bought it specially to please a particular person.

SHUI TA: As things have turned out that is no longer necessary.

WANG *makes a sling out of the shawl*: She is my only witness.

THE POLICEMAN: Your cousin is supposed to have seen Shu Fu the barber strike the water-carrier with his curling-tongs. Do you know anything about that?

SHUI TA: I only know that my cousin was not present when this slight incident took place.

WANG: It's a misunderstanding! When Shen Teh comes she will clear it all up. Shen Teh will bear me out. Where is she?

SHUI TA, *seriously*: Mr Wang, you call yourself my cousin's friend. At the moment my cousin has really serious worries. She has been disgracefully exploited on all sides. From now on she cannot permit herself the slightest weakness. I am convinced that you will not ask her to ruin herself utterly by testifying in your case to anything but the truth.

WANG, *puzzled*: But she told me to go to the magistrate.

SHUI TA: Was the magistrate supposed to cure your hand?

THE POLICEMAN: No. But he was to make the barber pay up.

Mr Shu Fu turns round.

SHUI TA: Mr Wang, one of my principles is never to interfere in a dispute between my friends.

Shui Ta bows to Mr Shu Fu, who bows back.

WANG, *sadly, as he takes off the sling and puts it back*: I see.

THE POLICEMAN: Which means I can go, eh? You tried your game on the wrong man, on a proper gentleman that is. You be a bit more careful with your complaints next time, fellow. If Mr Shu Fu doesn't choose to waive his legal rights you can still land in the cells for defamation. Get moving!

Both exeunt.

SHUI TA: I beg you to excuse this episode.

MR SHU FU: It is excused. *Urgently*: And this business about a 'particular person?' *He points to the shawl.* Is it really over? Finished and done with?

SHUI TA: Completely. She has seen through him. Of course, it will take time for it all to heal.

MR SHU FU: One will be careful, considerate.

SHUI TA: Her wounds are fresh.

MR SHU FU: She will go away to the country.

SHUI TA: For a few weeks. But she will be glad to talk things over first with someone she can trust.

MR SHU FU: Over a little supper, in a small but good restaurant.

SHUI TA: Discreetly. I shall hasten to inform my cousin. She will show her good sense. She is greatly upset about her business, which she regards as a gift from the gods. Please be so good as to wait for a few minutes. *Exit into the back room.*

MRS SHIN *sticks her head in*: Can we congratulate you?

MR SHU FU: You can. Mrs Shin, will you tell Shen Teh's dependents from me before tonight that I am giving them shelter in my buildings across the yard?

She grins and nods.

MR SHU FU, *standing up, to the audience*: What do you think of me, ladies and gentlemen? Could one do more? Could one be more unselfish? More delicate? More far-sighted? A little supper. How crude and vulgar that would normally sound. Yet there will be nothing of that kind, not a thing. No contact, not even an apparently accidental touch when passing the salt. All that will happen will be an exchange of ideas. Two souls will discover one another, across the flowers on the table – white chrysanthemums, by the way. *He notes it down.* No, this will be no exploiting of an unfortunate situation, no profiting from a disappointment. Understanding and assistance will be offered, but almost unspoken. By a glance alone will they be acknowledged, a glance that can also signify rather more.

MRS SHIN: Has it all turned out as you wanted, Mr Shu Fu?

MR SHU FU: Oh, quite as I wanted. You can take it that there will be changes in this neighbourhood. A certain character has been sent packing, and one or two hostile movements against this shop are due to be foiled. Certain persons who have no hesitation in trampling on the good name of the most respectable girl in this town will in future have me to deal with. What do you know about this Yang Sun?

MRS SHIN: He is the idlest, dirtiest . . .

MR SHU FU: He is nothing. He does not exist. He is simply not present, Mrs Shin.

Enter Sun.

SUN: What's this about?

MRS SHIN: Would you like me to call Mr Shui Ta, sir? He won't like strangers wandering round the shop.

MR SHU FU: Miss Shen Teh is having an important discussion with Mr Shui Ta, and they cannot be interrupted.

SUN: She's here, is she? I didn't see her go in! What are they discussing? They can't leave me out!

MR SHU FU *prevents him from going into the back room*: You will have to be patient, sir. I think I know who you are. Kindly take note that Miss Shen Teh and I are about to announce our engagement.

SUN: What?

SHIN: That is a surprise for you, isn't it?

Sun struggles with the barber in an effort to get into the back room; Shen Teh emerges.

MR SHU FU: Forgive us, my dear Shen Teh. Perhaps you will explain.

SUN: What's up, Shen Teh? Have you gone crazy?

SHEN TEH, *breathlessly*: Sun, Mr Shu Fu and my cousin have agreed that I ought to listen to Mr Shu Fu's ideas of how to help the people round here. *Pause.* My cousin is against our relationship.

SUN: And you have agreed?

SHEN TEH: Yes.

Pause.

SUN: Have they told you I'm a bad character?

Shen Teh remains silent.

SUN: Perhaps I **am**, Shen Teh. And that is why I need you. I am a debased character. No capital, no manners. But I can put up a fight. They're wrecking your life, Shen Teh. *He goes up to her, subdued*: Just look at him! Haven't you got eyes in your head? *Putting his hand on her shoulder*: Poor creature, what are they trying to shove you into now? Into a sensible marriage! If it weren't for me they would simply have put you out of your misery. Tell me yourself: but for me, wouldn't you have gone off with him?

SHEN TEH: Yes.

SUN: A man you don't love!

SHEN TEH: Yes.

SUN: Have you completely forgotten? The rain?

SHEN TEH: No.

SUN: How you hacked me down from the tree, how you brought me a glass of water, how you promised me the money so I could fly again?

SHEN TEH, *trembling*: What do you want?

SUN: Come away with me.

SHEN TEH: Mr Shu Fu, forgive me, I want to go away with Sun.

SUN: We are in love, you know. *He escorts her to the door.* Have you got the key of the shop? *He takes it from her and gives it to Mrs Shin.* Put it on the step when you've finished. Come, Shen Teh.

MR SHU FU: But this is rape! *He shouts into the back room*: Mr Shui Ta!

SUN: Tell him not to make so much row here.

SHEN TEH: Please don't call my cousin, Mr Shu Fu. We are not of one mind, I know. But he is not in the right, I can sense it.
To the audience:
> I would go with the man whom I love.
> I would not reckon what it costs me.
> I would not consider what is wiser.
> I would not know whether he loves me.
> I would go with the man whom I love.

SUN: Just like that.

Both walk off.

INTERLUDE
in front of the curtain

Shen Teh in her wedding clothes, on her way to the wedding, turns and addresses the audience.

SHEN TEH: I have had a fearful experience. As I stepped out of the door, joyous and full of expectation, I found the carpet-dealer's old wife standing in the street, shakily telling me that her husband was so excited and troubled about the money she lent me that he had fallen ill. She thought it best for me in any case to give her back the money. Of course I promised. She was greatly relieved and, weeping, gave me her good wishes, begging me to excuse her for not completely trusting my cousin, nor, alas, Sun. I had to sit down on the steps when she left, I had so scared myself. In the tumult of my feelings I had thrown myself once more into Yang Sun's arms. I could resist neither his voice nor his caresses. The evil that he had spoken to Shui Ta could not teach Shen Teh a lesson. Sinking into his arms, I still thought; the gods wanted me to be kind to myself too.

> To let none go to waste, not oneself either
> To bring happiness to all, even oneself, that
> Is good.

How could I simply have forgotten the two good old people? Like a small hurricane Sun just swept my shop off in the direction of Pekin, and with it all my friends. But he is not evil, and he loves me. As long as I am near him he will do nothing wicked; what a man tells other men means nothing. He wants to seem big and strong then, and particularly hard-boiled. If I tell him that the old people cannot pay their taxes he will understand. He would rather get a job at the cement works than owe his flying to a wrong action. True, flying is a tremendous passion with him. Shall I be strong enough to call out the goodness in him? At the moment, on the way to my wedding, I am hovering between fear and joy.

She goes off quickly.

6

Private Room in a cheap Suburban Restaurant

A waiter is pouring out wine for the wedding guests. Round Shen Teh stand the grandfather, the sister-in-law, the niece, Mrs Shin and the unemployed man. A priest stands by himself in a corner. Sun is talking to his mother, Mrs Yang, in front. He is wearing a dinner jacket.

SUN: Bad news, mother. She just told me, oh so innocently, that she can't sell the shop for me. Some people are dunning her to pay back those 200 silver dollars she gave you. Though her cousin says there's nothing about it in writing.

MRS YANG: What did you say to her? You can't marry her, of course.

SUN: There's no point in discussing all that with her; she is too pig-headed. I have sent for her cousin.

MRS YANG: But he wants to get her married to the barber.

SUN: I've dealt with that marriage. The barber has been seen off. Her cousin will soon realise the business has gone if I don't produce the two hundred, as the creditors will seize it, but that the job's gone too if I don't get the 300 on top.

MRS YANG: I'll go and look for him outside. Go and talk to your bride now, Sun!

SHEN TEH, *to the audience as she pours out wine*: I was not mistaken in him. Not a line of his face betrayed disappointment. Despite the heavy blow that it must have been to renounce his flying he is perfectly cheerful. I love him very much. *She motions Sun to come to her.* Sun, you have not yet drunk with the bride!

SUN: What shall we drink to?

SHEN TEH: Let it be to the future.

They drink.

SUN: When the bridegroom's dinner jacket is his own!

SHEN TEH: But the bride's dress is still sometimes exposed to the rain.

SUN: To all we want for ourselves!

SHEN TEH: May it come soon!

MRS YANG, *to Mrs Shin as she leaves*: I am delighted with my son. I've always tried to make him realise that he can get any girl he wants. Him, a trained pilot and mechanic. And what does he go and tell me now? I am marrying for love, mother, he says. Money isn't everything. It's a love match! *To the sister-in-law*: Sooner or later these things have to happen, don't they? But it's hard on a mother, very hard. *Calling to the priest*: Don't cut it too short. If you take as long over the ceremony as you did arguing about the fee, that will make it nice and dignified. *To Shen Teh*: We shall have to hold things up a bit, my dear. One of our most valued guests has still to arrive. *To all*: Please excuse us. *Exit*.

THE SISTER-IN-LAW: It's a pleasure to be patient as long as there's something to drink.

They sit down.

THE UNEMPLOYED MAN: We're not missing much.

SUN, *loudly and facetiously in front of the guests*: Before the ceremony starts I ought to give you a little test. There's some point when the wedding's at such short notice. *To the guests*: I have no idea what sort of wife I'm going to get. It's most disturbing. For instance, can you use three tea-leaves to make five cups of tea?

SHEN TEH: No.

SUN: Then I shan't be getting any tea. Can you sleep on a straw mattress the size of that book the priest's reading?

SHEN TEH: Double?

SUN: Single.

SHEN TEH: In that case, no.

SUN: Dreadful, what a wife I'm getting.

All laugh. Behind Shen Teh Mrs Yang appears in the doorway. She shrugs her shoulders to tell Sun that the expected guest is not to be seen.

MRS YANG, *to the priest, who is pointing to his watch*: Don't be in such a hurry. It can't be more than a matter of minutes. There they are, all drinking and smoking, and none of them's in a hurry. *She sits down with her guests.*

SHEN TEH: But oughtn't we to discuss how it's all going to be settled?

MRS YANG: Now, not a word about business today. It so lowers the tone of a party, don't you think?

The bell at the door rings. All look towards the door, but nobody comes in.

SHEN TEH: Who is your mother waiting for, Sun?

SUN: It's to be a surprise for you. By the way, where is your cousin, Shui Ta? I get on well with him. A very sensible fellow! Brainy! Why don't you say something?

SHEN TEH: I don't know. I don't want to think about him.

SUN: Why not?

SHEN TEH: Because I wish you didn't get on with him. If you like me, you can't like him.

SUN: Then I hope the gremlins got him: the engine gremlin, the petrol gremlin and the fog gremlin. Drink, you old obstinate!

He forces her.

THE SISTER-IN-LAW, *to Mrs Shin*: Something fishy here.

MRS SHIN: What else did you expect?

THE PRIEST *comes firmly up to Mrs Yang, with his watch in his hand*: I must go, Mrs Yang. I've got a second wedding, and a funeral first thing in the morning.

MRS YANG: Do you imagine I'm holding things up for pleasure? We hoped that one jug of wine would see us through. Now look how low it's getting. *Loudly, to Shen Teh*: I can't understand, my dear Shen Teh, why your cousin should let us wait for him like this!

SHEN TEH: My cousin?

MRS YANG: But my dear girl, it's him we're waiting for. I am old-fashioned enough to feel that such a close relation of the bride ought to be at the wedding.

SHEN TEH: Oh Sun, is it about the 300 dollars?

SUN, *without looking at her*: You've heard what it's about. She is old-fashioned. I've got to consider her. We'll just wait a quarter of an hour, and if he hasn't come by then it'll mean the three gremlins have got him, and we'll start without!

MRS YANG: I expect you have all heard that my son is getting a position as a mail pilot. I am delighted about it. It's important to have a well-paid job in these days.

THE SISTER-IN-LAW: In Pekin, they say: is that right?

MRS YANG: Yes, in Pekin.

SHEN TEH: Sun, hadn't you better tell your mother that Pekin is off?

SUN: Your cousin can tell her if he feels the same way as you. Between you and me, I don't.

SHEN TEH, *shocked*: Sun!

SUN: God, how I loathe Szechwan! What a town! Do you realise what they all look like when I half shut my eyes? Like horses. They look up nervously: what's that thundering over their heads? What, won't people need them any more? Have they outlived their time? They can bite each other to death in their horse town! All I want is to get out of here!

SHEN TEH: But I promised the old couple I'd pay them back.

SUN: Yes, that's what you told me. And it's a good thing your cousin's coming as you're so silly. Drink your wine and leave business to us! We'll fix it.

SHEN TEH, *horrified*: But my cousin can't come!

SUN: What do you mean?

SHEN TEH: He's not there.

SUN: And how do you picture our future: will you kindly tell me?

SHEN TEH: I thought you still had the 200 silver dollars. We can pay them back tomorrow and keep the tobacco, which is worth much more, and sell it together outside the cement works as we can't pay the rent.

SUN: Forget it! Put it right out of your mind, sister! Me stand in the street and hawk tobacco to the cement workers: me, Yang Sun the pilot? I'd sooner blow the whole 200 in a single night. I'd sooner chuck it in the river! And your cousin knows me. I fixed with him he was to bring the 300 to the wedding.

SHEN TEH: My cousin cannot come.

SUN: And I thought he couldn't possibly stay away.

SHEN TEH: It is impossible for him to be where I am.

SUN: How very mysterious!

SHEN TEH: Sun, you must realise he is no friend of yours. It is I who love you. My cousin Shui Ta loves nobody. He is a friend to me, but not to my friends. He agreed that you should have the old people's money because he was thinking of your pilot's job in Pekin. But he will not bring the 300 silver dollars to the wedding.

SUN: And why not?

SHEN TEH, *looking him in the eyes*: He says you only bought one ticket to Pekin.

SUN: Yes, but that was yesterday, and look what I've got to show him today! *He half pulls two tickets out of his breast pocket.* There's no need for the old woman to see. That's two tickets to Pekin, for me and for you. Do you still think your cousin's against the marriage?

SHEN TEH: No. The job is a good one. And my business has gone.

SUN: It's for your sake I sold the furniture.

SHEN TEH: Don't say any more! Don't show me the tickets! It makes me too afraid that I might simply go off with you. But do you see, Sun, I can't give you the 300 silver dollars, or what is to become of the two old people?

SUN: What's to become of me? *Pause.* You'd better have a drink! Or do you believe in being careful? I can't stick a careful woman. When I drink I start flying again. And you: if you drink there's just the faintest shadow of a possibility you may understand me.

SHEN TEH: Don't think I don't understand you. You want to fly, and I can't be any help.

SUN: 'Here's your plane, beloved, but I'm afraid it's a wing short.'

SHEN TEH: Sun, there's no honourable way for us to get that

job in Pekin. That's why I need you to hand back the 200 silver dollars I gave you. Give them to me now, Sun!

SUN: 'Give them to me now, Sun!' What do you think you are talking about? Are you my wife or aren't you? Because you're ratting on me, don't you realise? Luckily – and luckily for you too – it doesn't depend on you, because it's all been settled.

MRS YANG, *icily*: Sun, are you certain the bride's cousin will be coming? It almost looks as though he had something against this marriage, as he doesn't appear.

SUN: But what are you thinking of, mother! Him and me are like that. I'll open the door wide so that he spots us at once as he comes rushing up to act as best man to his old friend Sun. *He goes to the door and kicks it open. Then he comes back, swaying slightly because he has already drunk too much, and sits down again by Shen Teh.* We'll wait. Your cousin has got more sense than you. Love is an essential part of living, he wisely says. And what's more he knows what it would mean for you: no shop left and no wedding either!

They wait.

MRS YANG: At last!

Footsteps are heard, and all look towards the door. But the footsteps move on.

MRS SHIN: There's going to be a scandal. One can feel it; one can sniff it in the air. The bride is waiting for the ceremony, but the bridegroom is waiting for her honourable cousin.

SUN: The honourable cousin is taking his time.

SHEN TEH, *softly*: Oh, Sun!

SUN: Sitting here with the tickets in my pocket, and an idiot beside me who can't do arithmetic! And I see the day coming when you'll be putting the police on me to get your 200 silver dollars back.

SHEN TEH, *to the audience*: He is evil and he would like me to be evil too. Here am I who love him, and he stays waiting for a cousin. But round me sit the defenceless: the old woman with her sick husband, the poor who wait at the door every morning for rice, and an unknown man from Pekin who is worried about his job. And they all protect me because they all have faith in me.

SUN *stares at the glass jug in which the wine is near the bottom*: The wine-jug is our clock. We are poor people, and once the guests have drunk the wine the clock has run down for ever.

Mrs Yang signs to him to keep silent, and footsteps can be heard once more.

THE WAITER *enters*: Do you wish to order another jug of wine, Mrs Yang?

MRS YANG: No, I think there will be enough. Wine only makes one too hot, don't you think?

MRS SHIN: I imagine it costs a lot too.

MRS YANG: Drinking always makes me perspire.

THE WAITER: Would you mind settling the bill now, madam?

MRS YANG *ignores him*: Ladies and gentlemen, I hope you can be patient a little longer: our relative must be on his way by now. *To the waiter*: Don't interrupt the party.

THE WAITER: My orders are not to let you leave until the bill is settled.

MRS YANG: But I am well known here!

THE WAITER: Exactly!

MRS YANG: The service nowadays is really outrageous! Don't you think so, Sun?

THE PRIEST: I fear that I must leave. *Exit weightily*.

MRS YANG, *desperate*: Please all of you remain seated! The priest will be back in a few minutes.

SUN: Drop it, mother. Ladies and gentlemen, now that the priest has left we cannot detain you any longer.

THE SISTER-IN-LAW: Come on, Grandpa!

THE GRANDFATHER *solemnly empties his glass*: The bride!

THE NIECE, *to Shen Teh*: Don't mind him. He means it friendly-like. He's fond of you.

MRS SHIN: That's what I call a flop!

All the guests leave.

SHEN TEH: Shall I leave too, Sun?

SUN: No, you wait. *He pulls at her wedding finery so that it is askew.* It's your wedding, isn't it? I'm going to wait on, and the old lady will wait on. She is anxious to see her bird in the air again anyhow. It's my opinion that the moon will be nothing but green cheese before she can step outside and see his plane thundering over the house. *To the empty chairs as if the guests were still there*: Ladies and gentlemen, can't you make conversation? Don't you like it here? The wedding has only been somewhat postponed, on account of the non-arrival of influential relations, and because the bride doesn't know what love is. To keep you amused I, the bridegroom, will sing you a song. *He sings*:

THE SONG OF GREEN CHEESE

A day will come, so the poor were informed
As they sat at their mother's knees
When a child of low birth shall inherit the earth
And the moon shall be made of green cheese.
　　When the moon is green cheese
　　The poor shall inherit the earth.

Then goodness will be a thing to reward
And evil a mortal offence.
'Where there's merit there's money' won't sound quite
　　　　so funny
There will really be no difference.
　　When the moon is green cheese
　　There won't be this difference.

Then the grass will look down on the blue sky below
And the pebbles will roll up the stream
And man is a king. Without doing a thing
He gorges on honey and cream.
　　When the moon is green cheese
　　The world flows with honey and cream.

Then I shall become a pilot again
And you'll get a deputy's seat.
You, man on the loose, will find you're some use
And you, ma, can put up your feet.
    When the moon is green cheese
    The weary can put up their feet.

And as we have waited quite long enough
This new world has got to be born
Not at the last minute so there's nothing left in it
But at the first glimmer of dawn
    When the moon is green cheese
    The very first glimmer of dawn.

MRS YANG: He won't come now.

The three of them sit there and two of them look towards the door.

INTERLUDE

Wang's Sleeping Place

Once more the gods appear to the water-seller in a dream. He has fallen asleep over a large book. Music.

WANG: How good that you have come, Illustrious Ones! Permit me a question which disturbs me greatly. In the tumbledown hut belonging to a priest who has left to become an unskilled labourer in the cement works I discovered a book, and in it I found a remarkable passage. I should like to read it to you. It runs: *With his left hand he thumbs through an imaginary book laid over the book in his lap, and lifts this imaginary book up to read from it, leaving the real one lying where it was.* 'In Sung there is a place known as Thorn Hedge. There catalpas, cypresses and mulberries flourish. Now those trees which are nine or ten inches in circumference are chopped down by the people who need stakes for their dog kennels. Those which are three or four feet in circumference are chopped down by rich and respectable families who want planks for their coffins. Those which are seven or eight feet in circumference are chopped down by persons seeking beams for their luxurious villas. And so none reaches its full quota of years, but is brought down prematurely by saw or by axe. That is the price of utility.'

THE THIRDGOD: That would mean that the least useful is the best.

WANG: No, only the most fortunate. The least good is the most fortunate.

THE FIRST GOD: Ah, what things they write!

THE SECOND GOD: Why are you so deeply moved by this comparison, O water-seller?

WANG: On account of Shen Teh, Illustrious Ones! She has failed in her love because she obeyed the commandment to love her neighbours. Perhaps she really is too good for this world, O Illustrious Ones!

THE FIRST GOD: Nonsense. You poor, feeble creature! It seems to me that you are half eaten away by scepticism and lice.

WANG: Certainly, O Illustrious One! I only thought you might perhaps intervene.

THE FIRST GOD: Out of the question. Our friend here – *he points to the third god, who has a black eye* – intervened in a quarrel only yesterday; you see the result.

WANG: But they had to send for her cousin yet again. He is an unusually capable man, I know from experience, but even he could not set things straight. It looks as if the shop were already lost.

THE THIRD GOD, *disturbed*: Do you think perhaps we ought to help?

THE FIRST GOD: My view is that she has got to help herself.

THE SECOND GOD, *strictly*: The worse the difficulties, the better the good man will prove to be. Suffering ennobles!

THE FIRST GOD: We are putting all our hopes in her.

THE THIRD GOD: Our search is not progressing well. Now and again we come across a good start, admirable intentions, a lot of high principles, but it hardly adds up to a good person.

When we do find people who are halfway good, they are not
living a decent human existence. *Confidentially*: The nights
are getting worse and worse. You can tell where we have
been spending them from the straws sticking to our clothes.

WANG: Just one request. Could you not at least . . .

THE GODS: Nothing. We are but observers. We firmly believe
that our good person will find her own feet on this sombre
earth. Her powers will wax with her burden. Only wait a
little, O water-seller, and you will find all's well that ends . . .

*The gods' figures have been growing steadily paler, their voices
steadily fainter. Now they disappear, and their voices cease.*

7

Yard behind Shen Teh's Shop

*A few household goods on a cart. Shen Teh and Mrs Shin are
taking washing down from the line.*

MRS SHIN: I can't think why you don't put up a better fight for
your business.

SHEN TEH: How? I can't even pay the rent. I have got to pay
the old people their 200 silver dollars back today, and because
I've given them to someone else I shall have to sell my stock
to Mrs Mi Tzu.

MRS SHIN: All gone, eh? No man, no stock, no home! That
comes of trying to set oneself up as a cut above our lot. How
do you propose to live now?

SHEN TEH: I don't know. I might earn a bit as a tobacco sorter.

MRS SHIN: What are Mr Shui Ta's trousers doing here? He
must have gone off in his shirt.

SHEN TEH: He's got another pair.

MRS SHIN: I thought you said he had gone away for good. What
does he want to leave his trousers behind for?

SHEN TEH: Perhaps he's finished with them.

MRS SHIN: Oughtn't you to make a parcel of them?

SHEN TEH: No.

Mr Shu Fu bursts in.

MR SHU FU: Don't tell me. I know it all. You have sacrificed your young love so that two old people who trusted you should not be ruined. It was not for nothing that this malicious and mistrustful district christened you 'The Angel of the Slums'. The gentleman to whom you were engaged proved unable to raise himself to your moral stature; you threw him over. And now you are closing your shop, that little haven of refuge for so many! I cannot stand by and see it. Day after day I have stood at the door of my shop and seen the knot of down-and-outs before your window, and you yourself doling out rice. Must all that vanish for ever? Must goodness be defeated? Ah, if only you will allow me to assist you in your good works! No, don't say a thing! I wish for no assurances. No promises that you will accept my help! But herewith – *he takes out a cheque-book and writes a cheque, which he lays on the cart* – I make you out a blank cheque, which you can fill in for any sum you like; and now I shall go, quietly and modestly, demanding nothing in return, on tiptoe, full of respectful admiration, not a thought for myself.

Exit.

MRS SHIN *examines the cheque*: This'll save you! People like you have some luck! You can always find a mug. Now hurry up. Write in 1,000 silver dollars and I'll run to the bank with it before he comes to his senses.

SHEN TEH: Put the laundry basket on the cart. I can pay for the washing without that cheque.

MRS SHIN: What do you mean? You're not going to take the cheque? That's criminal! Is it just because you feel you would have to marry him? That would be plain crazy. A fellow like that just asks to be led by the nose! That sort really likes it. Are you still wanting to hang on to that pilot of yours, when everyone here and in Yellow Alley knows how badly he's treated you?

SHEN TEH: It all comes from poverty. *To the audience*:

At night I watched him blow out his cheeks in his sleep: they were evil

And at dawn I held his coat up to the light, and saw the
    wall through it.
When I saw his sly smile I was afraid, but
When I saw the holes in his shoes I loved him dearly.

MRS SHIN: So you're still sticking up for him? I never heard
anything so idiotic. *Angry*: I shall be relieved when we have
got you out of the district.

SHEN TEH *staggers as she takes down the washing*: I'm feeling a
bit giddy.

MRS SHIN *takes the washing from her*: Do you often feel giddy
when you bend or stretch? Let's only hope it isn't a little
one! *Laughs*. He has fixed you good and proper! If that's it
then the big cheque will turn sour. It wasn't meant for that
sort of situation. *She goes to the rear with a basket.*

*Shen Teh looks after her without moving. Then she examines her
body, feels it, and a great joy appears in her face.*

SHEN TEH, *softly*: Oh joy! A small being is coming to life in my
body. There is nothing to see yet. But he is already there.
The world awaits him in secret. In the cities they have heard
the rumour: someone is coming now with whom we must
reckon. *She presents her small son to the audience*: An airman!
    Salute a new conqueror
    Of unknown mountains, inaccessible countries! One
    Carrying letters from man to man
    Across the wastes where no man yet has trod!
*She begins to walk up and down, leading her small son by the
hand.* Come my son, inspect your world. Here, that is a tree.
Bow politely, greet him. *She performs a bow.* There, now you
know one another. Listen, that is the water-seller coming. A
friend, shake hands with him. Don't be nervous. 'A glass of
cool water for my son, please. It's a hot day.' *She hands him
the glass.* Ah, the policeman! I think we will avoid him. Perhaps we might collect one or two cherries over th̶̶̶
rich old Mr Feh Pung's orchard. This is a mome̶̶̶
seen. Come, poor little bastard! You too like cherri̶̶̶
soft, my son! *They walk cautiously, looking around them.* No,

round this way, where the bushes will shield us. No, no going straight to the point in this case. *He seems to be dragging away; she resists.* We've got to be sensible. *Suddenly she gives in.* Very well, if you can't do it any other way. . . . *She lifts him up.* Can you reach the cherries? Shove them in your mouth, that's the best place for them. *She eats one herself, which he puts into her mouth.* Tastes fine. O god, the police. This is where we run. *They flee.* Here's the road. Now gently, walk slowly so we don't attract attention. As if nothing whatever had happened. . . . *She sings as she walks along with the child*:

> A plum off my tree
> Bit a man on the knee
> The man had a thirst
> Got his own bite in first.

Wang the water-seller has entered, leading a child by the hand. He watches Shen Teh in astonishment.

SHEN TEH, *as Wang coughs*: Oh, Wang! Good day.

WANG: Shen Teh, I have heard you are in difficulties, that you must even sell your business to pay debts. But here's this child without any home. It was playing about in the slaughter-house. They say it belongs to Lin To the carpenter, who had to give up his workshop a few weeks ago and is now on the drink. His children are wandering around starving. What can be done with them?

SHEN TEH *takes the child from him*: Come on, little man! *To the audience*:

> Here, you! Someone begging for shelter.
> A chip of tomorrow begging you for a today.
> His friend, the conqueror, whom you know
> Can answer for him.

To Wang: He can quite well live in Mr Shu Fu's sheds, where I may be going too. I myself am expecting a child. But do not repeat that, or Yang Sun may hear of it, and we can only hamper him. See if you can find Lin To in the lower town, and tell him to come here.

WANG: Many thanks, Shen Teh. I knew you would find an

answer. *To the child*: See? A good person always knows a way. I'll go off quickly and fetch your father. *He starts to go.*

SHEN TEH: Oh, Wang, I have just remembered. What happened about your hand? I did want to give evidence for you, but my cousin . . .

WANG: Don't bother about my hand. Look, I've already learnt to do without my right hand. I hardly need it at all. *He shows her how he can manage his carrying pole without his right hand*: See how I manage?

SHEN TEH: But you mustn't let it get stiff! Take that cart, sell the lot, and use the money to go to the doctor. I am ashamed of having let you down like that. And what must you think of me for accepting the barber's offer of the sheds!

WANG: The homeless can live there now, and you yourself. After all, that matters more than my hand. I'll go and fetch the carpenter. *Exit.*

SHEN TEH *calls after him*: Promise me you'll let me take you to the doctor!

Mrs Shin has come back and has been making repeated signs.

SHEN TEH: What is it?

MRS SHIN: Are you mad? Giving away the cart with all you've got left? What's his hand to do with you? If the barber gets to know he'll throw you out of the last lodging you're likely to find. You haven't paid me for the washing yet!

SHEN TEH: Why are you so unpleasant?

> To trample on one's fellows
> Is surely exhausting? Veins in your temples
> Stick out with the strenuousness of greed.
> Loosely held forth
> A hand gives and receives with the same suppleness. Yet
> Greedily snatching it has got to strain. Oh
> How tempting it is to be generous. How welcome
> Friendliness can somehow feel. A kindly word
> Escapes like a sigh of contentment.

Mrs Shin goes off angrily.

SHEN TEH, *to the child*: Sit here and wait till your father comes.

The child sits on the ground. Enter the elderly couple who visited Shen Teh on the day of the opening of her shop. Man and wife are dragging big sacks.

THE WOMAN: Are you by yourself, Shen Teh? *When Shen Teh nods she calls in her nephew, who is also carrying a sack.* Where's your cousin?

SHEN TEH: He went away.

THE WOMAN: Is he coming back?

SHEN TEH: No. I'm giving up the shop.

THE WOMAN: So we heard. That's why we've come. These are a few sacks of leaf tobacco which somebody owed us, and we'd be ever so grateful if you could move them to your new home with your own things. We've no place to put them yet, and if we have them in the street people are bound to notice. I don't see how you can refuse to do us this little favour after the bad luck we had in your shop.

SHEN TEH: I will do it for you gladly.

THE MAN: And if anyone happens to ask you whose sacks these are you can say they're yours.

SHEN TEH: Who would want to know?

THE WOMAN, *giving her a sharp look*: The police for one. They've got it in for us, and they're out to ruin us. Where do we put the sacks?

SHEN TEH: I don't know; just at this moment I'd sooner not do anything that might get me into gaol.

THE WOMAN: Isn't that like you? All we've been able to save of our things is a few rotten old sacks of tobacco, and a lot you care if we lose them!

Shen Teh is stubbornly silent.

THE MAN: Don't you see that this stock of tobacco might allow us to start manufacturing in a small way? Then we could work our way up.

SHEN TEH: All right, I'll keep your sacks for you. They can go in the back room for the present.

*She goes in with them. The child has been watching her. Now it
looks round timidly, goes to the dustbin and starts fishing in it. It
begins to eat something that it has found. Shen Teh and the others
return.*

THE WOMAN: You realise we're completely in your hands?

SHEN TEH: Yes. *She notices the child and stiffens.*

THE MAN. We'll call on you the day after tomorrow in Mr Shu
    Fu's buildings.

SHEN TEH: Please leave at once; I'm not well. *She pushes them
    out. Exeunt the three.* He's hungry. Fishing in the dustbin.

*She lifts up the child and expresses her horror at the fate of poor
children in a speech, showing the audience his dirty mouth. She
proclaims her determination never to treat her own child in such a
heartless way.*

O son, O airman! What sort of a world
Awaits you? Will you too
Be left to fish in the garbage? Observe
The greyness round his mouth! *She exhibits the child.* Is that
How you treat your fellow-creatures? Have you
Not the least compassion for the fruit
Of your bodies? No pity
For yourselves, you unfortunates? Henceforth I
Shall fight at least for my own, if I have to be
Sharp as a tiger. Yes, from the hour
When I saw this thing I shall cut myself off
From them all, never resting
Till I have at least saved my son, if only him.
What I learnt from my schooling, the gutter
By violence and trickery now
Shall serve you, my son: to you
I would be kind; a tiger, a savage beast
To all others if need be. And
It need be.

She goes off to change herself into her cousin.

SHEN TEH, *walking off*: Once more it must be done, for the last time I hope.

She has taken Shui Ta's trousers with her. Mrs Shin returns and stares inquisitively after her. Enter the sister-in-law and the grandfather.

THE SISTER-IN-LAW: Shop shut, all her stuff in the yard! It's the finish!

MRS SHIN: That's what comes of selfishness, irresponsibility and the lusts of the flesh! And where is she heading? Downwards! To Mr Shu Fu's sheds, along with the rest of you!

THE SISTER-IN-LAW: She'll be surprised at what she finds there! We've come to complain! A damp rabbit-warren with half rotten floors! The barber only let us have them because his stock of soap was going bad there. 'I can give you shelter, what do you say to that?' We say, it's a scandal!

Enter the unemployed man.

THE UNEMPLOYED MAN: Is it true Shen Teh's clearing out?

THE SISTER-IN-LAW: Yes. She meant to sneak away so we shouldn't know.

MRS SHIN: She's ashamed because she's broke.

THE UNEMPLOYED MAN, *excited*: She must send for her cousin! All of you, advise her to send for her cousin! He's the only one can do anything.

THE SISTER-IN-LAW: That's right! He's mean enough, but at least he'll save her business, and then she'll be generous.

THE UNEMPLOYED MAN: I wasn't thinking of us, I was thinking of her. But it's a fact: he must be sent for for our sakes too.

Enter Wang with the carpenter. He is leading two children by the hand.

THE CARPENTER: Truly, I can't thank you enough. *To the others*: We're to get a lodging.

MRS SHIN: Where?

THE CARPENTER: In Mr Shu Fu's buildings. And it was little Feng who managed it! Ah, there you are! 'Here's someone begging for shelter', Miss Shen Teh's supposed to have said, and she finds us lodgings there and then. Say thank you to your brother, all of you!

The carpenter and his children make pretence of bowing to the child.

THE CARPENTER: Our thanks, shelter-beggar!

Shui Ta has entered.

SHUI TA: May I ask what you are all doing here?
THE UNEMPLOYED MAN: Mr Shui Ta!
WANG: Good day, Mr Shui Ta. I didn't realise you were back. You know Lin To the carpenter. Miss Shen Teh promised to find him a corner in one of Mr Shu Fu's buildings.
SHUI TA: Mr Shu Fu's buildings are booked.
THE CARPENTER: Does that mean we can't lodge there?
SHUI TA: No. These premises are reserved for another purpose.
THE SISTER-IN-LAW: Have we got to move out too then?
SHUI TA: Unfortunately.
THE SISTER-IN-LAW: But where can we all go?
SHUI TA, *shrugging his shoulders*: Miss Shen Teh, who has left town, gave me to understand that she had no intention of neglecting you. In future however it must all be rather more sensibly arranged. No more free meals without working for it. Instead every man shall have the opportunity to improve his condition honourably by his labour. Miss Shen Teh has decided to find work for you all. Those of you who now choose to follow me into Mr Shu Fu's buildings will not be led into the blue.
THE SISTER-IN-LAW: Do you mean we've all got to start working for Shen Teh?
SHUI TA: Yes. You will shred tobacco. There are three full bales in the back room there. Get them!
THE SISTER-IN-LAW: Don't forget we used to have a shop of our own. We'd rather work for ourselves. We've got our own tobacco.
SHUI TA, *to the unemployed man and the carpenter*: Perhaps you

would like to work for Shen Teh, as you have no tobacco of your own?

The carpenter and the unemployed man comply reluctantly, and exeunt. Mrs Mi Tzu enters.

MRS MI TZU: Now then, Mr Shui Ta, how about the sale of the stock? I have your 300 silver dollars here with me.

SHUI TA: Mrs Mi Tzu, I have decided not to sell, but to sign the lease.

MRS MI TZU: What? Don't you want the money for the pilot any more?

SHUI TA: No.

MRS MI TZU: And can you find the rent?

SHUI TA *takes the barber's cheque off the cart and fills it in.* I have here a cheque for 10,000 silver dollars, signed by Mr Shu Fu, who is taking an interest in my cousin. Look for yourself, Mrs Mi Tzu! You will get your 200 silver dollars for the next half-year's rent before six this evening. And now, Mrs Mi Tzu, you will allow me to go on with my own work. I am extremely busy today and must ask you to excuse me.

MRS MI TZU: So Mr Shu Fu is in the pilot's shoes now! 10,000 silver dollars! All the same I am astounded that young girls nowadays should be so frivolous and unstable, Mr Shui Ta. *Exit.*

The carpenter and the unemployed man bring in the sacks.

THE CARPENTER: I can't think why I should have to cart your sacks for you.

SHUI TA: The point is that I can. Your son has a healthy appetite. He wants to eat, Mr Lin To.

THE SISTER-IN-LAW *sees the sacks*: Has my brother-in-law been here?

MRS SHIN: Yes.

THE SISTER-IN-LAW: I thought so. I know those sacks. That's our tobacco.

SHUI TA: I advise you not to say that so loudly. That is my tobacco, as you can see from the fact that it was in my room.

But if you have any doubts about it we can go to the police
and clear them up. Do you wish to?

THE SISTER-IN-LAW, *crossly*: No.

SHUI TA: Evidently you haven't got your own stock of tobacco
after all. Perhaps under those circumstances you will accept
the helping hand which Miss Shen Teh is offering you? Be
so good now as to show me the way to Mr Shu Fu's buildings.

*Taking the hand of the carpenter's youngest child, Shui Ta walks
off, followed by the carpenter, his remaining children, the sister-in-
law, the grandfather, the unemployed man. Sister-in-law, carpenter
and unemployed man drag out the sacks.*

WANG: He is not a wicked man, but Shen Teh is good.

MRS SHIN: I'm not sure. There's a pair of trousers missing from
the clothes line, and her cousin is wearing them. That must
mean something. I'd like to know what.

Enter the two old people.

THE OLD WOMAN: Is Miss Shen Teh not here?

MRS SHIN, *absently*: Left town.

THE OLD WOMAN: That's strange. She was going to bring us
something.

WANG, *looking painfully at his hand*: And she was going to help
me. My hand's going stiff. She's sure to be back soon. Her
cousin never stays long.

MRS SHIN: He doesn't, does he?

INTERLUDE

Wang's Sleeping Place

Music. In a dream the water-seller informs the gods of his fears. The gods are still engaged on their long pilgrimage. They seem tired. Unresponsive at first, they turn and look back at the water-seller.

WANG: Before you appeared and awoke me, O Illustrious Ones, I was dreaming and saw my dear sister Shen Teh in great distress among the reeds by the river, at the spot where the suicides are found. She was staggering in a strange way and held her head bent as if she were carrying something soft and heavy that was pressing her into the mud. When I called to her she called back that she must carry the whole bundle of precepts across to the other bank, keeping it dry so that the ink should not run. In fact I could see nothing on her shoulder. But I was sharply reminded that you gods had lectured her about the major virtues as a reward for her taking you in when you were stuck for a night's lodging, the more shame to us! I am certain you understand my worries for her.

THE THIRD GOD: What do you suggest?

WANG: A slight reduction of the precepts, Illustrious Ones. A slight alleviation of the bundle of precepts, O gracious ones, in view of the difficulty of the times.

THE THIRD GOD: For instance, Wang, for instance?

WANG: For instance, that only good will should be required instead of love, or . . .

THE THIRD GOD: But that is far harder, you unhappy man!

WANG: Or fairness instead of justice.

THE THIRD GOD: But that means more work!

WANG: Then plain decency instead of honour!

THE THIRD GOD: But that is far more, you man of doubts!

They wander wearily on.

8

Shui Ta's Tobacco Factory

Shui Ta has set up a small tobacco factory in Mr Shu Fu's huts.
Horribly constricted, a number of families huddle behind bars.
Women and children predominate, among them the sister-in-law,
the grandfather, the carpenter and his children. In front of them
enter Mrs Yang, followed by her son, Sun.

MRS YANG, *to the audience*: I must describe to you how the
  wisdom and discipline of our universally respected Mr Shui
  Ta turned my son Sun from a broken wreck into a useful
  citizen. Near the cattle-yard, as the whole neighbourhood
  quickly came to hear, Mr Shui Ta started a small but rapidly
  prospering tobacco factory. Three months ago I found it
  advisable to call on him there with my son. He received me
  after a brief wait.

Shui Ta comes up to Mrs Yang from the factory.

SHUI TA: What can I do for you, Mrs Yang?
MRS YANG: Mr Shui Ta, I should like to put in a word for my
  son. The police came round this morning, and we heard that
  you were suing in Miss Shen Teh's name for breach of
  promise and fraudulent conversion of 200 silver dollars.
SHUI TA: Quite correct, Mrs Yang.
MRS YANG: Mr Shui Ta, in the gods' name can you not temper
  justice with mercy once more? The money has gone. He ran
  through it in a couple of days as soon as the idea of the pilot's
  job fell through. I know he is a bad lot. He had already sold
  my furniture and was going to set off to Pekin without his
  poor old mother. *She weeps.* There was a time when Miss
  Shen Teh thought very highly of him.
SHUI TA: Have you got anything to say to me, Mr Yang Sun?
SUN, *sombrely*: The money's gone.
SHUI TA: Mrs Yang, in view of the weakness which my cousin
  for some inexplicable reason felt for your broken-down son,
  I am prepared to give him another chance. She told me she

thought honest work might bring an improvement. I can find him a place in my factory. The 200 silver dollars will be deducted in instalments from his wages.

SUN: So it's to be factory or clink?

SHUI TA: It's your own choice.

SUN: And no chance of talking to Shen Teh, I suppose.

SHUI TA: No.

SUN: Show me where I work.

MRS YANG: A thousand thanks, Mr Shui Ta. Your kindness is overwhelming, and the gods will repay you. *To Sun*: You have strayed from the narrow path. See if honest work will make you fit to look your mother in the face again.

Sun follows Shui Ta into the factory. Mrs Yang returns to the front of the stage.

MRS YANG: The first weeks were difficult for Sun. The work was not what he was used to. He had little chance to show what he could do. It was only in the third week that a small incident brought him luck. He and Lin To who used to be a carpenter were shifting bales of tobacco.

Sun and the former carpenter Lin To are each shifting two bales of tobacco.

THE FORMER CARPENTER *comes to a halt groaning, and lowers himself on to one of the bales*: I'm about done in. I'm too old for this sort of work.

SUN *likewise sits down*: Why don't you tell them they can stuff their bales?

THE FORMER CARPENTER: How would we live then? To get the barest necessities I must even set the kids to work. A pity Miss Shen Teh can't see it! She was good.

SUN: I've known worse. If things had been a bit less miserable we'd have hit it off quite well together. I'd like to know where she is. We had better get on. He usually comes about now.

They get up.

SUN *sees Shui Ta coming*: Give us one of your sacks, you old cripple! *Sun adds one of Lin To's bales to his own load.*

THE FORMER CARPENTER: Thanks a lot! Yes, if she were there you'd certainly go up a peg when she saw how helpful you were to an old man. Ah yes!

Enter Shui Ta.

MRS YANG: And a glance is enough for Mr Shui Ta to spot a good worker who will tackle anything. And he takes a hand.

SHUI TA: Hey, you two! What's happening here? Why are you only carrying one sack?

THE FORMER CARPENTER: I feel a bit run down today, Mr Shui Ta, and Yang Sun was so kind . . .

SHUI TA: You go back and pick up three bales, my friend. If Yang Sun can do it, so can you. Yang Sun puts his heart in it, and you don't.

MRS YANG, *while the former carpenter fetches two more bales*: Not a word to Sun, of course, but Mr Shui Ta had noticed. And next Saturday, at the pay desk . . .

A table is set up and Shui Ta comes with a small bag of money. Standing next the overseer – the former unemployed man – he pays out the wages. Sun steps up to the table.

THE OVERSEER: Yang Sun – 6 silver dollars.

SUN: Sorry, but it can't be more than five. Not more than 5 silver dollars. *He takes the list which the overseer is holding.* Look, here you are, you've got me down for six full days, but I was off one day, as I had to go to court. *Ingratiatingly*: I wouldn't like to be paid money I hadn't earned, however lousy the pay is.

THE OVERSEER: 5 silver dollars, then! *To Shui Ta*: Very unusual that, Mr Shui Ta!

SHUI TA: How do you come to have six days down here when it was only five?

THE OVERSEER: Quite correct, Mr Shui Ta, I must have made a mistake. *To Sun, coldly*: It won't occur again.

SHUI TA *calls Sun aside*: I have noticed lately that you have plenty of strength and don't grudge it to the firm. Now I see

that you are to be trusted too. Does it often happen that the
overseer makes mistakes to the firm's loss?

SUN: He's friends with some of the workers, and they count him
as one of them.

SHUI TA: I see. One good turn deserves another. Would you
like a bonus?

SUN: No. But perhaps I might point out that I have also got a
brain. I have had a fair education, you know. The overseer
has the right ideas about the men, but being uneducated he
can't see what's good for the firm. Give me a week's trial,
Mr Shui Ta, and I think I can prove to you that my brains
are worth more to the firm than the mere strength of my
muscles.

MRS YANG: They were bold words, but that evening I told my
Sun: 'You are a flying man. Show that you can get to the top
where you are now! Fly, my eagle!' And indeed it is remarkable what brains and education will achieve! How can a man
hope to better himself without them? Absolute miracles were
performed by my son in the factory directed by Mr Shui Ta!

*Sun stands behind the workers, his legs apart. They are passing a
basket of raw tobacco above their heads.*

SUN: Here you, that's not proper work! The basket has got to
be kept moving! *To a child*: Sit on the ground, can't you?
It takes up less room! And you might as well get on with a
bit of pressing: yes, it's you I'm talking to! You idle loafers,
what do you think you're paid for? Come on with that basket!
O hell and damnation! Put grandpa over there and let him
shred with the kids! There's been enough dodging here!
Now take your time from me! *He claps time with his hands
and the basket moves faster.*

MRS YANG: And no enmities, no slanderous allegations by the
uneducated – for he was not spared that – could hold my son
back from the fulfilment of his duty.

*One of the workers begins singing the song of the eighth elephant.
The others join in the chorus.*

WORKERS' CHORUS:

SONG OF THE EIGHTH ELEPHANT

I

Seven elephants worked for Major Chung
And an eighth one followed the others.
Seven were wild and the eighth was tame
And the eighth had to spy on his brothers.
> Keep moving!
> Major Chung owns a wood
> See it's cleared before tonight.
> That's orders. Understood?

2

Seven elephants were clearing the wood
The eighth bore the Major in person
Number eight merely checked that the work was correct
And spared himself any exertion.
> Dig harder!
> Major Chung owns a wood
> See it's cleared before tonight.
> That's orders. Understood?

3

Seven elephants got tired of their work
Of shoving and digging and felling.
The Major was annoyed with the seven he employed
But rewarded the eighth one for telling.
> What's up now?
> Major Chung owns a wood
> See it's cleared before tonight.
> That's orders. Understood?

4

Seven elephants, not a tusk in their heads
The eighth's were in excellent order.
So eight used his wits, slashed the seven to bits
And the Major had never laughed harder.

Dig away!
Major Chung owns a wood
See it's cleared before tonight
That's orders. Understood?

Shui Ta has lounged forward, smoking a cigar. Yang Sun has laughingly joined in the chorus of the third verse and quickened the tempo in the fourth verse by clapping his hands.

MRS YANG: We really owe everything to Mr Shui Ta. With wisdom and discipline, but with hardly a word of interference, he has brought out all the good that lay in Sun! He made no fantastic promises like his much overrated cousin, but forced him to do good honest work. Today Sun is a different person from what he was three months ago. I think you will admit it! 'The noble soul is like a bell, strike it and it rings, strike it not and it rings not', as our forebears used to say.

9
Shen Teh's Shop

The shop has been turned into an office, with easy chairs and fine carpets. It is raining. Shui Ta, now become fat, is showing out the old couple of carpet-dealers. Mrs Shin watches with amusement. It is plain that she is wearing new clothes.

SHUI TA: I regret that I cannot say when she will be back.
THE OLD WOMAN: We had a letter today enclosing the 200 silver dollars we once lent her. It didn't say who from. But it can only be Shen Teh who sent it. We'd like to write to her: what's her address?
SHUI TA: I'm afraid I don't know that either.
THE OLD MAN: We'd better go.
THE OLD WOMAN: Sooner or later she is bound to come back.

Shui Ta bows. The two old people go off uncertain and upset.

MRS SHIN: It was too late when they got their money back. Now they've lost their shop because they couldn't pay their taxes.

SHUI TA: Why didn't they come to me?

MRS SHIN: People don't like coming to you. I expect they started by waiting for Shen Teh to come back as they'd got nothing in writing. Then the old man got ill at the critical moment, and his wife had to nurse him night and day.

SHUI TA *has to sit down because he feels sick*: I feel giddy again.

MRS SHIN *fusses around him*: You're six months gone! You mustn't let yourself get worked up. Lucky for you you've got me. Everyone can do with a helping hand. Yes, when your time comes I shall be at your side. *She laughs.*

SHUI TA, *feebly*: Can I count on that, Mrs Shin ?

MRS SHIN: You bet! It'll cost money of course. Undo your collar, and you'll feel better.

SHUI TA, *pitifully*: It's all for the baby's sake, Mrs Shin.

MRS SHIN: All for the baby's sake.

SHUI TA: I'm getting fat so quickly, though. People are bound to notice.

MRS SHIN: They think it's because you're doing so well.

SHUI TA: And what will happen to him?

MRS SHIN: You're always asking that. He will be looked after. The best that money can buy.

SHUI TA: Yes. *Anxiously*: And he must never see Shui Ta.

MRS SHIN: Never. Only Shen Teh.

SHUI TA: But all the gossip round here! The water-seller and his rumours! They're watching the shop!

MRS SHIN: As long as the barber doesn't hear there's no harm done. Come on dear, have a drop of water.

Enter Sun in a smart suit carrying a business man's brief-case. He is amazed to see Shui Ta in Mrs Shin's arms.

SUN: Am I disturbing you?

SHUI TA *gets up with difficulty and goes unsteadily to the door*: Till tomorrow, then, Mrs Shin!

Mrs Shin puts on her gloves and goes off smiling.

SUN: Gloves! How, why, what for? Is she milking you? *On Shui Ta not replying*: Don't tell me even you have your softer moments. Curious. *He takes a document from his brief-case.* Anyway, you haven't been on form lately, not on your old form. Moody. Hesitant. Are you ill? It's doing no good to the business. Here's another notice from the police. They want to shut the factory. They say they can't possibly allow more than twice the legal number of people to a room. It's about time you took some action, Mr Shui Ta!

Shui Ta looks at him distractedly for a moment. Then he goes into the back room and returns with a box. He takes out a new bowler and throws it on the table.

SHUI TA: The firm wishes its representatives to dress according to their position.

SUN: Did you get that for me?

SHUI TA, *indifferently*: See if it fits.

Sun looks astounded, then puts it on. Shui Ta tries adjusting it at the right angle.

SUN: At your service, sir. But don't try and dodge the question. You must see the barber today and talk about the new scheme.

SHUI TA: The barber makes impossible conditions.

SUN: I wish you'd tell me what conditions.

SHUI TA, *evasively*: The sheds are quite good enough.

SUN: Good enough for the riffraff who work there, but not good enough for the tobacco. The damp's getting in it. Before we have another meeting I'll see Mrs Mi Tzu again about her premises. If we can get them we can chuck out this rag, tag and bobtail. They're not good enough. I'll tickle Mrs Mi Tzu's fat knees over a cup of tea, and we'll get the place for half the money.

SHUI TA, *sharply*: That is out of the question. For the sake of the firm's reputation I wish you always to be coolly business-like, and to be reserved in personal matters.

SUN: What are you so irritable for? Is it the unpleasant local gossip?

SHUI TA: I am not concerned with gossip.

SUN: Then it must be the weather again. Rain always makes you so touchy and melancholic. I'd like to know why.

WANG'S VOICE, *from without*:

> I sell water. Who would taste it?
> – Who would want to in this weather?
> All my labour has been wasted
> Fetching these few pints together.
> I stand shouting Buy my Water!
> And nobody thinks it
> Worth stopping and buying
> Or greedily drinks it.

SUN: There's that bloody water-seller. Now he'll be nagging us again.

WANG'S VOICE, *from without*: Isn't there a good person left in this town? Not even on the square where the good Shen Teh used to live? Where is the woman who once bought a mug of water from me in the rain, months ago, in the joy of her heart? Where is she now? Has nobody seen her? Has none of you heard from her? This is the house which she entered one evening and never left!

SUN: Hadn't I better shut his mouth for good? What's it got to do with him, where she is? Incidentally, I believe the only reason why you don't say is so that I shouldn't know.

WANG *enters*: Mr Shui Ta, I ask you once more: when is Shen Teh coming back? It's now six months since she went off on her travels. *On Shui Ta remaining silent*: Since then a lot has happened which could never have taken place if she'd been here. *On Shui Ta still remaining silent*: Mr Shui Ta, the rumour round here is that something must have happened to Shen Teh. Her friends are very worried. Would you please be so good as to let us know her address?

SHUI TA: I fear I have no time at the moment, Mr Wang. Come again next week.

WANG, *worked up*: People have also begun to notice that the rice she used to give the needy is being put out at the door again.

SHUI TA: What do they conclude from that?

WANG: That Shen Teh hasn't gone away at all.

SHUI TA: But? *On Wang's remaining silent*: In that case I will give you my answer. It is final. If you consider yourself a friend of Shen Teh's, Mr Wang, then you will refrain from enquiring as to her whereabouts. That is my advice.

WANG: Marvellous advice! Mr Shui Ta, Shen Teh told me before she disappeared that she was pregnant!

SUN: What?

SHUI TA, *quickly*: A lie!

WANG, *most seriously*, *to Shui Ta*: Mr Shui Ta, please don't think Shen Teh's friends will ever give up the search for her. A good person is not easily forgotten. There are not many. *Exit.*

Shui Ta stares after him. Then he goes quickly into the back room.

SUN, *to the audience*: Shen Teh pregnant! That makes me livid! I've been done! She must have told her cousin, and of course that swine hurried her off at once. 'Pack your bags and clear out, before the child's father gets wind of it!' It's utterly against nature. Inhuman, in fact. I've got a son. A Yang is about to appear on the scene! And what happens? The girl vanishes, and I'm left here to work like a slave. *He is losing his temper.* They buy me off with a hat! *He tramples on it.* Crooks! Thieves, kidnappers! And the girl has nobody to look after her! *Sobbing is heard from the back room. He stops still.* Wasn't that someone crying? Who's there? It's stopped. What's that crying in the back room? I bet that half-baked swine Shui Ta doesn't cry. So who's crying? And what's the meaning of the rice being put outside the door every morning? Is the girl there after all? Is he simply hiding her? Who else could be crying in there? That would be a fine kettle of fish! I've absolutely got to find her if she's pregnant!

Shui Ta returns from the back room. He goes to the door and peers out into the rain.

SUN: Well, where is she?

SHUI TA *raises his hand and listens*: Just a moment! Nine o'clock. But one can't hear today. The rain is too heavy.

SUN, *ironically*: What do you hope to hear?

SHUI TA: The mail plane.

SUN: Don't be funny.

SHUI TA: I thought they told me you were interested in flying? Have you dropped that?

SUN: I have no complaints about my present job, if that's what you mean. I'd sooner not do night work, you know. The mail service means flying at night. I've begun to get a sort of soft spot for the firm. After all, it is my former fiancée's firm, even if she is away. She did go away, didn't she?

SHUI TA: Why do you ask?

SUN: Maybe because her affairs don't leave me entirely cold.

SHUI TA: My cousin might like to hear that.

SUN: Anyway I'm concerned enough to be unable to shut my eyes if I find, for instance, that she is being deprived of her freedom.

SHUI TA: By whom?

SUN: By you!

Pause.

SHUI TA: What would you do in such an eventuality?

SUN: I might start by wanting to reconsider my position in the firm.

SHUI TA: Indeed. And supposing the firm – that is to say I – found a suitable position for you, would it be able to count on your giving up all further enquiries about your former fiancée?

SUN: Possibly.

SHUI TA: And how do you picture your new position in the firm?

SUN: Full control. For instance, I picture chucking you out.

SHUI TA: And suppose the firm chucked you out instead?

SUN: Then I should probably return, but not on my own.

SHUI TA: But?

SUN: With the police.

SHUI TA: With the police. Let us suppose the police found no one here.

SUN: Then I presume they would look in that room! Mr Shui

Ta, my longing for the lady of my heart cannot be suppressed. I feel I shall have to take steps if I am to enfold her in my arms once more. *Quietly*: She's pregnant, and needs a man beside her. I must talk it over with the water-seller. *He leaves.*

Shui Ta looks after him without moving. Then he goes quickly into the back room once more. He fetches all kinds of everyday articles of Shen Teh's: underwear, dresses, toilet things. He looks lengthily at the shawl which Shen Teh bought from the old carpet-dealers. Then he packs it all into a bundle and hides it under the table, as he hears sounds. Enter Mrs Mi Tzu and Mr Shu Fu. They greet Shui Ta and dispose of their umbrellas and galoshes.

MRS MI TZU: Autumn's on the way, Mr Shui Ta.

MR SHU FU: A melancholy time of year!

MRS MI TZU: And where is that charming manager of yours? A shocking lady-killer! But of course you don't know that side of him. Still, he knows how to reconcile his charm with his business obligations, so you only profit from it.

SHUI TA *bows*: Will you please sit down?

They sit and start smoking.

SHUI TA: My friends, an unpredictable eventuality, which may have certain consequences, compels me to speed up the negotiations which I have recently initiated as to the future of my business. Mr Shu Fu, my factory is in difficulties.

MR SHU FU: It always is.

SHUI TA: But now the police are frankly threatening to shut it down if I cannot show that I am negotiating for a new arrangement. Mr Shu Fu, what is at stake is nothing less than the sole remaining property of my cousin, in whom you have always shown such interest.

MR SHU FU: Mr Shui Ta, it is deeply repugnant to me to discuss your ever-expanding projects. I suggest a small supper with your cousin, you indicate financial difficulties. I offer your cousin buildings for the homeless, you use them to set up a factory. I hand her a cheque, you cash it. Your cousin vanishes, you ask for 100,000 silver dollars and tell me my buildings are not big enough. Sir, where is your cousin?

SHUI TA: Mr Shu Fu, please be calm. I can now inform you that she will very shortly be back.

MR SHU FU: 'Shortly.' When? You have been saying 'shortly' for weeks.

SHUI TA: I have not asked you to sign anything further. I have simply asked whether you would be more closely associated with my project supposing my cousin came back.

MR SHU FU: I have told you a thousand times that I am not prepared to go on discussing with you, but will discuss anything with your cousin. However, you seem to want to put obstacles in the way of such a discussion.

SHUI TA: Not now.

MR SHU FU: Can we fix a date?

SHUI TA, *uncertainly*: In three months.

MR SHU FU, *irritably*: Then you can have my signature in three months too.

SHUI TA: But it must all be prepared.

MR SHU FU: You can prepare everything yourself, Shui Ta, if you are sure this time that your cousin really is coming.

SHUI TA: Mrs Mi Tzu, are you for your part ready to certify to the police that I can have your workshops?

MRS MI TZU: Certainly, if you will let me take over your manager. I told you weeks ago that that was my condition. *To Mr Shu Fu*: The young man is so conscientious, and I must have someone to run things.

SHUI TA: Please understand that I cannot let Mr Yang Sun go at this moment: there are all these problems, and my health has been so uncertain lately. I was always prepared to let you have him but . . .

MRS MI TZU: Ha! But!

Pause

SHUI TA: Very well, he shall report at your office tomorrow.

MR SHU FU: I am glad you could arrive at this decision, Mr Shui Ta. If Miss Shen Teh really comes back it will be most undesirable that this young man should be here. We all know that in his time he has had a most pernicious influence on her.

SHUI TA, *bowing*: No doubt. Forgive my undue hesitation in these questions relating to my cousin Shen Teh and Mr Yang Sun: it was quite unworthy of a business man. These two were once very close to each other.

MRS MI TZU: We forgive you.

SHUI TA, *looking towards the door*: My friends, it is time for us to come to a decision. At this spot, in what used to be the drab little shop where the poor of the district bought the good Shen Teh's tobacco, we, her friends, herewith resolve to establish twelve fine new branches, which from now on shall retail Shen Teh's good tobacco. I am told that people have begun calling me the Tobacco King of Szechwan. But the fact is that I have conducted this enterprise solely and exclusively in my cousin's interest. It will belong to her, and to her children, and to her children's children.

From without come sounds of a crowd of people. Enter Wang, Sun and the policeman.

THE POLICEMAN: Mr Shui Ta, I am extremely sorry, but in view of the disturbed state of the district I have to follow up certain information received from your own firm, according to which you are alleged to be keeping your cousin Miss Shen Teh under illegal restraint.

SHUI TA: That is not true.

THE POLICEMAN: Mr Yang Sun here states that he heard crying from the room behind your office, and that it can only have proceeded from a female person.

MRS MI TZU: That is absurd. Mr Shu Fu and I, two respected citizens of this town whose word the police can hardly doubt, will witness that there has been no crying here. We have been smoking our cigars perfectly quietly.

THE POLICEMAN: I'm afraid I have an order to search the aforementioned room.

Shui Ta opens the door. The policeman bows and crosses the threshold. He looks in, then turns round and smiles.

THE POLICEMAN: Perfectly true, there's no one there.

SUN, *who has accompanied him*: But someone was crying! *His eye falls on the table under which Shui Ta shoved the bundle. He pounces on it.* That wasn't there before!

He opens it and reveals Shen Teh's clothes, etc.

WANG: Those are Shen Teh's things! *He runs to the door and calls out*: They've found her clothes!

THE POLICEMAN, *taking charge of things*: You state that your cousin is away. A bundle containing her property is found concealed beneath your desk. Where can the young lady be contacted, Mr Shui Ta?

SHUI TA: I don't know her address.

THE POLICEMAN: That is a great pity.

SHOUTS FROM THE CROWD: Shen Teh's things have been found! The Tobacco King did the girl in and got rid of her!

THE POLICEMAN: Mr Shui Ta, I must ask you to come to the station with me.

SHUI TA, *bowing to Mrs Mi Tzu and to Mr Shu Fu*: Please forgive this disturbance, my dear colleagues. But we still have magistrates in Szechwan. I am sure it will all be cleared up quickly.

He precedes the policeman out.

WANG: There has been a most frightful crime!

SUN, *overcome*: But I did hear somebody crying!

INTERLUDE
Wang's Sleeping-Place

Music. For the last time the gods appear to the water-seller in a dream. They are greatly changed. It is impossible to mistake the symptoms of prolonged travel, utter exhaustion and unhappy experiences of every kind. One of them has had his hat knocked off his head, one has lost a leg in a fox-trap, and all three are going barefoot.

WANG: At last you have appeared! Fearful things are happening in Shen Teh's shop, Illustrious Ones! Shen Teh has again been away, this time for months! Her cousin has been grabbing everything! Today they arrested him. He is supposed to have murdered her in order to get hold of her shop. But I cannot believe that, for I had a dream in which she appeared to me and said that her cousin was keeping her a prisoner. Oh, Illustrious Ones, you must come back at once and find her.

THE FIRST GOD: That is terrible. Our whole search has been in vain. We found few good people, and those we found were not living a decent human existence. We had already decided to settle on Shen Teh.

THE SECOND GOD: If only she is still good!

WANG: That she surely is, but she has vanished!

THE FIRST GOD: Then all is lost!

THE SECOND GOD: You forget yourself.

THE FIRST GOD: What's wrong with forgetting oneself? We shall have to give up if she cannot be found! What a world we have found here: nothing but poverty, debasement and dilapidation! Even the landscape crumbles away before our eyes. Beautiful trees are lopped off by cables, and over the mountains we see great clouds of smoke and hear the thunder of guns, and nowhere a good person who survives it!

THE THIRD GOD: Alas, water-seller, our commandments seem to be fatal! I fear that all the moral principles that we have evolved will have to be cancelled. People have enough to do to save their bare lives. Good precepts bring them to the edge of the precipice; good deeds drag them over. *To the other gods*: The world is unfit to live in, you have got to admit it!

THE FIRST GOD, *emphatically*: No, mankind is worthless!

THE THIRD GOD: Because the world is too chilling!

THE SECOND GOD: Because men are too feeble!

THE FIRST GOD: Remember your dignity, my friends! Brothers, we cannot afford to despair. We did discover one who was good and has not become evil, and she has only disappeared. Let us hasten to find her. One is enough. Did we not say that all could still be redeemed if just one can be found who stands up to this world, just one?

They swiftly disappear.

10

Courtroom

In groups: Mr Shu Fu and Mrs Mi Tzu. Sun and his mother. Wang, the carpenter, the grandfather, the young prostitute, the two old people. Mrs Shin. The policeman. The sister-in-law.

THE OLD WOMAN: He is too powerful.

WANG: He means to open twelve new branches.

THE CARPENTER: How can the magistrate give a fair verdict when the defendant's friends, Shu Fu the barber and Mrs Mi Tzu the property owner, are his friends too?

THE SISTER-IN-LAW: Last night old Shin was seen carrying a fat goose into the judge's kitchen on Mr Shui Ta's orders. The grease was oozing through the basket.

THE OLD WOMAN, *to Wang*: Our poor Shen Teh will never be found again.

WANG: Yes, it will take the gods to get at the truth.

THE POLICEMAN: Silence! The court is assembling.

The three gods appear in magistrates' robes. As they pass along the front of the stage to go to their places they can be heard whispering.

THE THIRD GOD: There will be trouble. The certificates were most incompetently forged.

THE SECOND GOD: And people will be curious about the magistrate's sudden indisposition.

THE FIRST GOD: It is natural enough after eating half a goose.

MRS SHIN: We've got new magistrates!

WANG: And very good ones!

The third god, last of the three, hears him, turns and smiles at him. The gods take their seats. The first god taps on the table with a hammer. The policeman brings in Shui Ta, who is received with catcalls but maintains an air of arrogance as he enters.

THE POLICEMAN: This may be a shock to you. Fu Yi Cheng is not on the bench. But the new magistrates look pretty soft too.

Shui Ta catches sight of the gods and faints.

THE YOUNG PROSTITUTE: What's happened? The Tobacco King has fainted.

THE SISTER-IN-LAW: As soon as he saw the new magistrates!

WANG: He seems to know them! That's beyond me.

THE FIRST GOD: Are you Shui Ta, tobacco merchant?

SHUI TA, *very faintly*: Yes.

THE FIRST GOD: You are charged with having made away with your cousin Miss Shen Teh, in order to gain control of her business. Do you plead guilty?

SHUI TA: No.

THE FIRST GOD, *thumbing through the papers*: The court will begin with the local constable's evidence as to the characters of the accused and his cousin.

THE POLICEMAN *steps forward*: Miss Shen Teh was a girl who made herself pleasant to everyone – live and let live, as they say. Mr Shui Ta, on the other hand, is a man of principle. The young lady's warm-hearted nature sometimes drove him to strict measures. But unlike the girl he was always on the side of the law, your worships. There were some people whom his cousin had trusted and taken in, and he was able to show them up as a gang of thieves, and another time he barely managed to save Shen Teh from straight perjury. Mr Shui Ta is known to me as a respectable citizen who respects the law.

THE FIRST GOD: Are there other witnesses in court who wish to testify that the accused is incapable of a crime of the sort attributed to him?

Mr Shu Fu and Mrs Mi Tzu step forward.

THE POLICEMAN *whispers to the gods*: Mr Shu Fu, one of our more prominent citizens!

MR SHU FU: The town looks up to Mr Shui Ta as an able business man. He is vice-chairman of the chamber of commerce and has been proposed as a justice of the peace.

WANG, *interrupting*: By you! You two are hand in glove with him.

THE POLICEMAN, *whispering*: An undesirable character!

MRS MI TZU: In my capacity as Chairman of the Charitable Welfare Association I should like to point out to the court that Mr Shui Ta is not only turning over the best possible rooms in his tobacco works – all light and healthy – to a considerable number of the homeless, but also makes regular subscriptions to our Disabled Persons' Institution.

THE POLICEMAN, *whispering*: Mrs Mi Tzu, a close friend of our magistrate Fu Yi Cheng!

THE FIRST GOD: Yes, yes, but now we must also hear whether anyone has a less favourable report to make on the accused.

There step forward: Wang, the carpenter, the old couple, the unemployed man, the sister-in-law, the young prostitute.

THE POLICEMAN: The scum of the district.

THE FIRST GOD: Tell us, what do you know of Shui Ta's general conduct?

CRIES, *confusedly*: He ruined us! He bled me white! Led us into bad ways! Exploited the helpless! Lied! Swindled! Murdered!

THE FIRST GOD: Accused, what have you to say for yourself?

SHUI TA: All I did was to save my cousin's bare means of existence, your worships. I only came when she was in danger of losing her small business. Three times I had to come. I never meant to stay. Circumstances were such that last time I was forced to remain. All the time I have had nothing but trouble. They loved my cousin, and I had to do the dirty work. That is why they hate me.

THE SISTER-IN-LAW: You bet we do. Look at our boy, your worships. *To Shui Ta*: Not to mention the sacks.

SHUI TA: Why not? Why not?

THE SISTER-IN-LAW, *to the gods*: Shen Teh put us up, and he had us arrested.

SHUI TA: You were stealing cakes!

THE SISTER-IN-LAW: Now he's pretending he cared about the baker and his cakes! He wanted the shop for himself!

SHUI TA: The shop wasn't a dosshouse, you selfish brutes!

THE SISTER-IN-LAW: But we had nowhere to go!

SHUI TA: There were too many of you!

WANG: And these two! *He points to the old couple.* Are they also too selfish?

THE OLD WOMAN: We put our savings into Shen Teh's business. Why did you do us out of our own?

SHUI TA: Because my cousin was helping an airman to get back into the air again. I was supposed to find the money!

WANG: She may have wanted that, but you had your eye on that good job in Pekin. The shop wasn't good enough for you.

SHUI TA: The rent was too high!

MRS SHIN: I can confirm that.

SHUI TA: And my cousin had no idea of business.

MRS SHIN: That too! Besides, she was in love with the airman.

SHUI TA: Hadn't she the right to love?

WANG: Of course she had! So why did you try to make her marry a man she didn't love: the barber there?

SHUI TA: The man she loved was a crook.

WANG: Him?

He indicates Sun.

SUN *leaps up*: Was it because he was a crook you took him into your office?

SHUI TA: To help you! To help you improve!

THE SISTER-IN-LAW: To turn him into a slave-driver!

WANG: And when you had finished improving him, didn't you
sell him to her? *He indicates Mrs Mi Tzu.* She was crowing
all over the place about it!

SHUI TA: Because she wouldn't let me have her workshops
unless he tickled her knees!

MRS MI TZU: Lies! Don't ever mention my workshops again!
I'll have nothing more to do with you. Murderer!

She rushes off in a dudgeon.

SUN, *firmly*: Your worships, I must put in a word for him!

THE SISTER-IN-LAW: You've got to; he's your boss.

THE UNEMPLOYED MAN: He's the worst slave-driver there ever
was. They completely broke him.

SUN: Your worships, whatever the accused made of me he is
not a murderer. A few minutes before his arrest I heard Shen
Teh's voice from the room behind the shop!

THE FIRST GOD, *intrigued*: She was alive, was she? Describe
exactly what you heard.

SUN, *triumphantly*: Crying, your worships, crying!

THE THIRD GOD: You could recognise it?

SUN: Absolutely certain. Don't I know her voice?

MR SHU FU: Yes, you've made her cry often enough!

SUN: But I've also made her happy. And then he wanted – *pointing to Shui Ta* – to sell her to you.

SHUI TA, *to Sun*: Because you didn't love her!

WANG: No: for the money!

SHUI TA: But what was the money needed for, your worships?
To Sun: You would have liked her to give up all her friends,
but the barber offered his buildings and his money so that
she could help the poor. I had to promise her to the barber
even to allow her to do good.

WANG: Why didn't you allow her to do good when the big
cheque was filled in? Why did you shove Shen Teh's friends
in your stinking sweat-shops, your tobacco factory, you
tobacco king?

SHUI TA: It was for the child's sake!

THE CARPENTER: And what about my children? What did you do to them?

Shui Ta remains silent.

WANG: That has made you think! The gods gave Shen Teh her shop to be a little source of goodness. And she always tried to do good, and you always came and brought it to nothing.

SHUI TA, *beside himself*: Because they'd have stifled the source, you fool.

MRS SHIN: That's quite true, your worships!

WANG: What's the good of a source that can't be drawn on?

SHUI TA: Good deeds are the road to ruin!

WANG, *wildly*: And evil deeds are the road to the good life, I suppose? What have you done with the good Shen Teh, you evil man? How many good people are there left, Illustrious Ones? She was certainly good! When that barber broke my hand she wanted to give evidence for me. And now I'm giving evidence for her. She was good, I swear it.

He raises his hand to swear.

THE THIRD GOD: What is wrong with your hand, water-seller? It seems stiff.

WANG *points to Shui Ta*: He's to blame, no one else! She was going to give me the money for the doctor, then he came along. You were her mortal enemy!

SHUI TA: I was her only friend!

ALL: Where is she?

SHUI TA: Gone away.

WANG: Where to?

SHUI TA: I shan't tell!

ALL: What made her go?

SHUI TA, *screaming*: You were tearing her to bits!

There is a sudden silence.

SHUI TA *has collapsed on to his chair*: I can't go on. If the court can be cleared so that only the magistrates are present I will make a confession.

ALL: Confession! We've won!

THE FIRST GOD *taps on the table with his hammer*: Clear the court.

The policeman clears the court.

MRS SHIN, *as she goes out, laughing*: They've got a surprise coming!

SHUI TA: Have they gone? All of them? I cannot hold out any longer. Illustrious Ones, I have recognised you!

THE SECOND GOD: What have you done with our good person of Szechwan?

SHUI TA: Let me confess the frightful truth. I am your good person!

He takes off his mask and rips away his costume. Shen Teh stands there.

THE SECOND GOD: Shen Teh!
SHEN TEH:
Yes, it is me. Shui Ta and Shen Teh, I am both of them.
Your original order
To be good while yet surviving
Split me like lightning into two people. I
Cannot tell what occurred: goodness to others
And to myself could not both be achieved.
To serve both self and others I found too hard.
Oh, your world is arduous! Such need, such desperation!
The hand which is held out to the starving
Is quickly wrenched off! He who gives help to the lost
Is lost for his own part! For who could
Hold himself back from anger when the hungry are dying?
Where could I find so much that was needed, if not
In myself? But that was my downfall! The load of commandments
Forced me into the sludge. Yet if I broke the rules
I strode proudly around, and could eat myself full!
Something is wrong with this world of yours. Why
Is wickedness so rewarded, and why is so much suffering

Reserved for the good? Oh, I felt such
Temptation to treat myself kindly! I felt too
A secret awareness inside me, for my foster-mother
Washed me with slops from the gutter! So I acquired
A sharp eye. And yet pity
Brought me such pain that I at once felt wolfish anger
At the sight of misery. Then
I could feel how I gradually altered and
My lips grew tight and hard. Bitter as ashes
The kind word felt in my mouth. And yet
I should gladly have been an Angel to the slums. For giving
Was still my delight. A smiling face
And I walked in the clouds.
Condemn me: each of my crimes
Was committed to help out my neighbour
To love my beloved or
To save my young son from going without.
O gods, for your vast projects
I, poor human, was too small.

THE FIRST GOD, *with every indication of horror*: Speak no further, you unhappy creature! What are we to think, who so rejoice to have found you again?

SHEN TEH: But do you not understand that I am the wicked person whose many crimes you have heard described?

THE FIRST GOD: The good person, of whom no one speaks anything but good!

SHEN TEH: No, the wicked person as well!

THE FIRST GOD: A misunderstanding! A few unfortunate incidents. One or two hard-hearted neighbours! A little too much zeal!

THE SECOND GOD: But how is she to go on living?

THE FIRST GOD: She can manage! She is strong, healthy and well-built, and can endure much.

THE SECOND GOD: But didn't you hear what she said?

THE FIRST GOD, *emphatically*: Muddled, completely muddled! Hard to accept, extremely hard to accept! Are we to admit that our commandments are fatal? Are we to sacrifice them?

Grimly: Never! Is the world to be altered? How? By whom?
No, everything is as it should be.

*He taps rapidly on the table with his hammer. And now – at a sign
from him – music is heard. A rosy glow is seen.*

> Now we return to heaven. This little world
> Still fascinates us. All its joys and hurts
> Encouraged us or caused us pain. And still
> We'll gladly think, away beyond the planets
> Of you, Shen Teh, the good person we sought
> Who makes our spirit manifest down here
> And through this bitter darkness bears the tiny lamp.
> Farewell, good luck!

*At a sign from him the ceiling opens. A pink cloud descends. On it
the three gods mount slowly upwards.*

SHEN TEH: Oh no, Illustrious Ones! Do not go away! Don't
leave me! How am I to face the two good old people who lost
their shop, or the water-seller with his stiff hand? And how
can I protect myself against the barber, whom I don't love,
and how against Sun, whom I do? And my body has been
blessed; soon my little son will be there and wanting to eat.
I cannot remain here!

*She looks frantically towards the door through which her tormentors
will come.*

THE FIRST GOD: You can manage. Only be good, and all will
be well!

*Enter the witnesses. They are amazed to see the magistrates floating
on their pink cloud.*

WANG: Show your respect! The gods have appeared among us!
Three of the mightiest gods have come to Szechwan in
search of a good person. They thought they had found one,
but . . .
THE FIRST GOD: No but! Here she is!
ALL: Shen Teh!

THE FIRST GOD: She was not dead, she lay but hidden. She will remain among you, a good person!

SHEN TEH: But I must have my cousin!

THE FIRST GOD: Not too often!

SHEN TEH: Once a week anyway!

THE FIRST GOD: Once a month: that will be enough!

SHEN TEH: Oh, do not go away, Illustrious Ones! I haven't told you all! I need you terribly!

THE GODS *sing*:

TRIO OF THE VANISHING GODS
ON THEIR CLOUD

All too long on earth we lingered.
Swiftly droops the lovely day:
Shrewdly studied, closely fingered
Precious treasures melt away.
Now the golden flood is dying
While your shadows onward press
Time that we too started flying
Homeward to our nothingness.

SHEN TEH: Help!

THE GODS:

Now let us go: the search at last is o'er
We have to hurry on!
Then give three cheers, and one cheer more
For the good person of Szechwan!

As Shen Teh stretches desperately towards them they disappear upwards, waving and smiling.

EPILOGUE

*A player appears before the curtain and addresses the audience
apologetically in an epilogue:*

THE PLAYER:

Ladies and gentlemen, don't feel let down:
We know this ending makes some people frown.
We had in mind a sort of golden myth
Then found the finish had been tampered with.
Indeed it is a curious way of coping:
To close the play, leaving the issue open.
Especially since we live by your enjoyment.
Frustrated audiences mean unemployment.
Whatever optimists may have pretended
Our play will fail if you can't recommend it.
Was it stage fright made us forget the rest?
Such things occur. But what would you suggest?
What is your answer? Nothing's been arranged.
Should men be better? Should the world be changed?
Or just the gods? Or ought there to be none?
We for our part feel well and truly done.
There's only one solution that we know:
That you should now consider as you go
What sort of measures you would recommend
To help good people to a happy end.
Ladies and gentlemen, in you we trust:
There must be happy endings, must, must, must!

Notes and Variants

Texts by Brecht

THE SONG FROM THE OPIUM DEN

1

THE GIRL

In those distant days of loving-kindness
Which they say are now forever gone
I adored the world, and sought for blindness
Or a heaven, the very purest one.
Soon enough, at dawn, I got my warning:
Blindness strikes the inquisitive offender
Who would see the heaven's pure bright dawning.
And I saw it. And I saw its splendour.
How can scrounging crumbs make people happy?
What's the good if hardships last for ever?
Must we never pluck the crimson poppy
Just because its blooms are sure to wither?
    And so I said: drop it.
    Breathe in the smoke twisting black
    Towards the colder heavens. Look up: like it
    You'll not come back.

2

THE MAN

My enemy who 'mid the poppies moulders–
I think of him when lighting up the drug.
And my bull? I've harnessed his great shoulders
And I've marched before a crimson flag.
By midday I'd tired of strife and rancour
Thought they offered nothing much to go on
You meantime were being so much franker
Saying they could be of use to no one.
Why smite enemies? I have no doubt mine
Nowadays could smite me without trying.
Nobody grows fatter than his outline.
Why, then, put on weight when you are dying?
    And so I said: drop it
    Breathe in the smoke twisting black
    Towards colder heavens. Look up: like it
    You'll not come back.

3

THE OLD MAN
    Ever since those distant days I've hurried
    Sown my millet, reaped it where it grew
    Lain with women, cried to gods when worried
    Fathered sons who now sow millet too.
    Late enough, at night, I got the lesson:
    Not a cock will crow, they're all ignoring
    My end – nor will the most complete confession
    Rouse a single god where he lies snoring.
    Why keep sowing millet on this gravel
    Soil whose barrenness can't be corrected
    If my tamarisk is doomed to shrivel
    Once I'm dead and it is left neglected?
        And so I said: drop it.
        Breathe in the smoke twisting black
        Towards colder heavens. Look up: like it
        You'll not come back.

> ['Der Gesang aus der Opiumhöhle,' GW *Gedichte*, pp. 90–91
> Brecht's typescript is dated by BBA 'About 1920.' This song,
> unpublished till after Brecht's death, is the origin of the 'Song
> of the Smoke' (pp. 19–20) and would appear to have been the
> first of his known writings on Chinese and Japanese themes.
> The opium motif will be found to recur in the Santa Monica
> version of the play (see pp. 121 - 126 and 132 ff.).]

FRAGMENT OF A STORY

However as the dearth increased and the cries of all living creatures
asserted themselves the gods grew uneasy. For there were many
complaints that there can be no fear of the gods where shortages are
excessive. And they said 'Were we to alter the world, which cost so
much effort to create, a great disorder would ensue. Therefore if we can
find people who are steadfast in time of dearth and keep our
commandments in spite of poverty then the world shall remain as it is
and there will be no disorder in it.'

Three of the highest thereupon set forth to discover god-fearing
people such as might keep their commandments and display resistance
in time of dearth.

And they came to the city of Szechwan, where they found a water seller who feared the gods, and he went around seeking a shelter for them. And he hunted round the city on their behalf for an entire day and could find no shelter.

And he said 'I thought that it would be simple, for these are among the highest of the gods, and it is only for one night. But there is not a house in Szechwan that will give them shelter.'

And he came back to them and comforted them, and went again and turned to a girl whom he knew by the name of Mi Lung to ask her for shelter.

And they saw that the measuring cup from which he sold water had a false bottom.

[From Werner Hecht (ed.): *Materialien zu Brechts 'Der gute Mensch von Sezuan,'* Frankfurt, Suhrkamp, 1968, p. 95. There described as 'probably written very early on.' The name Mi Lung never recurs.]

PRESS REPORT

A strange story has been reported from Szechwan province. Mr. Lao Go, a manufacturer of tobacco products in the provincial capital, has been standing trial for the murder of his cousin, a certain Miss Li Gung. According to witnesses this Miss Li Gung was known among the common populace of the slum quarters as a 'good person.' She even acquired the romantic sobriquet of 'angel of the slums.' Starting out as a simple woman of the streets, she was put in possession of a little capital by an alleged donation from the gods. She bought a tobacco shop, which however she ran on such altruistic lines that a few days later it was on the brink of ruin. Not only did she feed and maintain a number of persons from her extremely poor and overcrowded neighbourhood, but she also proved incapable of refusing lodging in her little shop to a family of nine with whom she was barely acquainted. Shortly before the débâcle a young man turned up describing himself to her numerous hangers-on as Miss Li Gung's cousin, and intervened so drastically as to put her confused affairs into comparative order. The following incident will provide an example of his methods. The family sent an adolescent boy out to steal bottles of milk from the neighbour's doorsteps. The cousin voiced no objection but called a policeman into the shop and chatted to him until the boy came back with the stolen milk. The visitors were forthwith taken off to the police station and Miss Li Gung was rid of them. The young lady for her part stayed away while her cousin was saving her business for her.

After her own return and her cousin Mr. Lao Go's departure, she resumed her charitable activities but on a very reduced scale. Instead she entered into an intimate relationship with an unemployed airmail pilot named Yü Schan whom she was locally rumoured to have saved from an attempted suicide. Unfortunately her hopes of making him a loan which would help him to secure a post as a mail pilot in Peking were cut short when her shop turned out not to be the little gold mine that people usually imagine such small concerns to be. There was a further threat to her shop in the shape of the methods employed by Mr. Feh Pung, the so-called 'Tobacco King of Szechwan,' a man not unduly inhibited by humanitarian scruples. When one of Mr. Feh Pung's shops opened in her immediate vicinity, selling tobacco fifty per cent cheaper, she once again bowed to outside advice and summoned her cousin to help. He did indeed . . . [A break in the typescript follows, during which there was presumably some mention of the other small tobacconists and their decision to unite.]

. . . On his first visit he had deliberately omitted to tell them of the threats already made to the shop by Feh Pung on the day of its opening; otherwise he would not have been admitted to their mutual aid association. While accepting their tobacco, which was intended to help him to hold out, he now nonetheless negotiated with Feh Pung and induced the tobacco king to make a special bid for the shop to the disadvantage of the other members. However, he was not anxious to effect his cousin's intended purchase of the desired post for her lover Yü Schan, even though the sale of the shop had put him in a position to do so. Apparently this Yü Schan had made it all too plain to him that he was counting on Li Gung's money. Rather than gratify Yü Schan's wishes her conscientious cousin arranged a sensible marriage between Mis Li Gung and the prosperous Mr. Kau, a barber. However, it seems that he had underestimated the extent of Yü Schan's power over his cousin. At any rate the pilot succeeded in gaining her complete confidence and persuading her to make a love marriage with himself. This marriage was much discussed in the neighbourhood, because it never came about. When the small tobacconists heard of Mr. Lao Go's plan to hand over the tobacco king Li Gung's shop, which had been kept afloat only by their joint efforts, they had little difficulty in persuading Li Gung to cancel it. Here her lover's power over her proved quite ineffective. Mr. Lao Go, sent for by the lover to make his cousin 'see reason,' failed to appear; then Li Gung realized how Schan's behaviour had hurt her, and made no secret of the fact that her cousin thought him a bad person and a fortune hunter; at which point the whole marriage blew up. Perhaps if the whole neighbourhood had not been so enchanted by its 'angel of the slums' it would by now have realised the amazing fact underlying the situation: that Mr. Lao Go was none other than Miss Li Gung herself. She was the conscientious 'cousin' whose sometimes equivocal manipulations made possible the good deeds for which people so admired her. However, it was to be a long time before Szechwan understood this. Unhappily the other tobacconists were not able to benefit from Li Gung's self-sacrifice. The short time spent on her efforts at marriage had been enough to make them doubt her loyalty. Undercutting one another's prices, they had handed their shops on a plate to the tobacco king, to the good old refrain of 'devil take the hindmost.' Li Gung meanwhile was forced to admit to her old friend Sun the water seller that she thought she was pregnant. The situation was desperate. Her shop was on the brink of total ruin. For the third (and, as it turned out, last) time her cousin appeared. His task was to rescue the shop on behalf of the expected child, object now of all the girl's love. The means selected by him were wholly unscrupulous. Taking every financial advantage both of the barber's admiration for his 'cousin' and the faith placed by many small people in the 'angel of the slums,' he organised a sweat shop of the worst sort in which her former friends and dependents were to process tobacco at starvation wages. Yü Schan, the child's father, was likewise roped into the rapidly booming business. Before her third disappearance Li Gung had promised his mother to find him a post where he might 'improve himself by honest work.' Under the strict hand of Mr. Lao Go he was made foreman in the new factory. The effect of such employment was to bring him into continual close contact with Mr. Lao Go. In the end this was to be Mr. Lao Go's downfall. Yü Schan had been led by an occasional small personal gift to believe that Mr. Lao Go was keeping his cousin locked up in a room at the back of the shop. He made an attempt at blackmail, which the tobacconist naturally rejected. Thwarted, he ended up by sending for the police, whereupon the back room proved to contain all Li Gung's clothing and personal possessions. The only way for Mr. Lao Go to answer the charge of murder was by making a clean breast of the true facts: that he and Miss Lil Gung were one and the same. Before the astonished eyes of the court, Lao Go changed back into Li Gung: the scourge of the slums and the angel of the slums were identical. Badness was only the reverse face of goodness, good deeds were made possible only by bad – a shattering testimonial to the unhappy condition of this world.

A poetic light is cast on the episode, which Szechwan regards as highly humorous, by the utterances of a water seller who claims that Li Gung's initial capital had indeed been a present from three gods, who told him that they had come to Szechwan to search for a good person, and also appeared more than once in his dreams to ask how the good person was faring. He claims that the three judges before whom the secret was finally unmasked were those same gods.

Whatever the real nature of the gods in question, they will no doubt have been somewhat surprised to find out in what way, in Szechwan, one sets about the problem of being a good person.

> [GW *Schriften zum Theater*, pp. 1157–61. Typescript is dated September 15, 1939, and in effect resumes the state of the story when Brecht abandoned it in order to write *Mother Courage*.]

WORKING PLAN

1. *swamped*

the little boat presented by the gods quickly fills with unfortunates to the point of capsizing / a family is given lodging / the former owners looked after / former suppliers arrive with demands / the landlady wants a guarantee /

2. *crisis and advertisement*

the cousin arrives to disentangle things / the family are handed over to the police / the suppliers paid off / the landlady placated / but as nastiness is neither a substitute for capital nor a shield against the powerful an advertisement must be drafted to get li gung a well-to-do husband.

3. *love*

quarrel about li gung's profession / she is off to an assignation with a well-to-do suitor / meets the unemployed pilot schan who is about to hang himself / comforts him / falls in love with him and buys him a glass of water from sun the water carrier /

4. *the flier has to fly*

sun's hand is broken / li gung tells of her love and buys a shawl / the barber falls desperately in love with her / but she discovers sun's wound and tries to find witnesses / without success / she offers to perjure herself / the carpet dealer and his wife overhear her talking to schan's mother about a job for schan which will cost 400 yen / they offer to guarantee the shop / the flier has to fly /

5. love triumphs

the cousin finds schan the money / sells the already mortgaged business to the landlady / gets to know schan and sees through him / talks things over with the barber / sun is disappointed / li gung should have a chance to do good / schan and the barber address the audience / li gung decides for schan /

6. the wedding

schan wants to get married and sell out / everybody is waiting for the cousin / the carpet dealers hurry in and are calmed by li gung / whenever li gung is present her cousin is not /

7. maternal joys

maternal joys / schan's mother / the guarantee / the garbage pail / the carpenter / li gung's little son will be looked after by her cousin /

8. the tobacco factory

the carpenter's children are hauling bales of tobacco / schan gets a job and distinguishes himself as foreman / song of the tobacco workers /

9. the rumour

rain / the landlady / schan makes a discovery / the monarchs smoke and the mob assembles / the police act /

10. the trial

the gods appear in the role of judges / the tobacco king is scared / the trial / the dénouement / the gods depart on a cloud /

[From Werner Hecht (ed.): *Materialien zu Brechts 'Der gute Mensch von Sezuan,'* Frankfurt, Suhrkamp, 1968, pp. 22–23. This is a typical big structural plan, probably dating from the summer of 1940 and used for the main work on the play, with the ten scenes set out in ten vertical columns across a wide sheet of paper. Under each Brecht has pencilled further notes and suggestions, of which Hecht provides a photographic reproduction and a transcription.]

UNDATED NOTES

1. Elements of the 'Good Person of Szechwan'

The gods' investigative commission   0, 10
A person's only friend: himself. The double role   4a
The good one takes the matter in hand; the bad one takes the matter
    in hand   1,2/ 4,5/ 5,6/ 7/ 8
Evil must come that good may come of it   1,2/ 4,5/ 5,6/ 7/ 8
The 'cousin' is always supposed to arrive just for a moment, or just once
    more, but in the end only he is the only one.   1, 4, 7
The gods don't find a good person, this is the best they can find   9 / 10
Lao Go's realisation of Schan's badness fails to cure Li Gung of her love
    for him.   5
The way of the little people: either up or down   10
The good person on trial: the gods on trail   10

2. Scenic elements of the 'Good Person of Szechwan'

How hard it is for a believer to give his gods what they want   0
How quickly goodness destroys a life   1
How quickly toughness builds a life up again   2
The good person seeks a helper and finds one that can be helped   3
Unfortunately only the cousin can help the loved one   4
But the cousin reveals the loved one's evil side. This of course is no help
    to the lover   5
Where Li Gung goes Lao Go cannot go   6
To help Li Gung's little son the cousin must sacrifice many other
    people's little sons   7
When Li Gung makes a promise Lao Go keeps his word   8
Has Lao Go murdered his cousin Li Gung?   9
The gods cross-examine the murderer of their good person   10

3. The good deeds of Li Gung

(i)   Sheltering a family
(ii)   Rescuring a desperate man
(iii)   Giving false evidence for a victim
(iv)   Confidence in the loved one
(v)   Confidence is not disappointed
(vii)   Underwriting ambition
(viii)   Everything for the child

4. The misdeeds of Lao Go

(ii)   Landing a family in prison
(iv)   Discrediting the victim
(v)   Letting down the underwriters
(vi)   Planning a 'marriage of convenience'
(vii)   Acquiring cheap premises
(viii)   Exploiting children
(ix)   Exploiting the loved one (The Tobacco Queen)

5. It is bad

to kill	8. The children	
to blackmail	7. Schan	
to abuse	5. the old couple	9. Schan
to let down	5. the old couple	5. Sun
to ruin	2. the family	7. the carpenter, the old couple
to lead astray	2. the family	
to exploit	8. all the helpless	
to repress	9. Schan	
to lie to		
to fäil to trust	9. Sun	
to despise	5. Schan	
to confuse	5. Sun	
to render unproductive	7. Caprenter	8. Schan
to make worse		
to neglect oneself		5.

[From Werner Hecht (ed.): *Materialien zu Brechts 'Der gute Mensch von Sezuan'.* Surkamp, Frankfurt, 1968, pp. 88–88]

LI GUNG'S BIG SPEECH ABOUT THE PUNISHMENT IMPOSED BY
THE GODS FOR FAILING TO EAT MEAT

The battles for food
Caused dreadful crimes. The brother
Drove his sister from the table. Married couples
Grabbed the plates from one another's hands. For one bit of meat
Son betrayed mother. Thus a sect arose
Which believed fasting would bring salvation. They said
None but the abstemious would remain human. He who longed
    to eat
Would inevitably decline into an animal. For a while
The best of them looked on the riches of our universe
As noxious filth. Then the gods stepped in.
Angered by this contempt for their gifts, they proclaimed the
    death penalty
For abstention. You could watch
How the non-eaters collapsed and grew hideous
And he who failed to eat meat died. To escape this terrible
    malady
People who fell on their food all the more greedily
Crime increased.

> [From Werner Hecht (ed.): *Materialien zu Brechts 'Der gute
> Mensch von Sezuan'*. Suhrkamp, Frankfurt, 1968, pp. 93–4.
> Cut passage included with an incomplete working typescript
> of summer 1940.]

FROM BRECHT'S JOURNAL

making minor corrections to *The Good Person* is costing me as many
weeks as writing the scenes did days. not easy, given the definite
objective, to imbue the tiny sub-scenes with that element of
irresponsibility, accident, transistoriness which we call 'life.' moreover
in the end there is a basic question to be settled: how to handle the *li
gung – lao go* problem. one can either (a) extend the parable aspect so
as to have a straightforward conflict, *gods – li gung – lao go*, which
would keep it all on a moral plane and allow two conflicting principles
('two souls') to figure separately, or else (b) have a plain story about
how *li gung* masquerades as her cousin and to that end makes use of
the experiences and qualities which her gutter existence has brought out
in her. in fact only (b) is possible unless one is to abandon mrs. shin's
discovery (scene 7), her conversation with the pregnant lao go and the
whole theme of how this pregnancy makes the double game impossible

to maintain. the transformation scene before the curtain (4a) is not in any way mystical but merely a technical solution in terms of mime and a song. where the difficulty becomes acute is wherever *lao go* directly addresses the audience the question is whether he ought not to do this using li gung's voice and consequently her attitude too. at bottom it all depends on how scene 5 is handled. this is where lao go must make some remark to explain his change of attitude. however, he has no confidant, nor can he make a confidant of the audience – not as lao go. What is more, li gung's collapse at the end of that scene is harder to understand if the solution adopted is (b) rather than (a). the only possible explanation is that here too she is being addressed as li gung. when you come down to it the elements *good* and *evil* are too segregated for a realistic drama of masquerade. an occasional slip would be unavoidable. the most realistic scene in this respect is the ninth. A further consideration could be that li gung has to make strenuous efforts to play the part of lao go and is no longer capable of appearing unpleasant when dressed in her own clothes and before the eyes of those who know and address her as li gung. herein lies an important lesson: how easy it is for her to be good and how hard to be evil.

[*Bertolt Brecht Arbeitsjournal*, vol. 1, 1938–42, Frankfurt, Suhrkamp, 1973, pp. 144–5. From the entry for August 9, 1940, roughly seven weeks after the completion of the first script and (obviously) before the changing of the characters' names. 'Two souls' is the Faustian concept also cited in *St Joan of the Stockyards*'.]

THE GOOD PERSON OF SZECHWAN

Prologue

Three gods enter the city of Szechwan. They are looking for a good person, having heard a rumour to the effect that to be good on this earth has become difficult. Aided by an obliging water seller they make the acquaintance of a good person, to wit the poor prostitute Chen Teh. Even she, however, complains that she finds it almost impossible to respect all the commandments of the gods, because she is so badly off. In order to give her a chance, the gods make her a present of money, convey their best wishes and leave her.

1

The good Chen Teh uses the gods' present of money to fit out a small tobacco shop. Concerned from the outset to obey the gods' commandments, to help her neighbours, to put her own interests second and to satisfy every request, no matter how far-fetched, from her none too good-natured fellow humans, she finds her shop close to riun the very evening after it has opened. A family of eight has chosen to take refuge there. To keep out further cadgers her "visitors'" cynically advise her to invent a cousin who will supposedly be a hard man and the real owner of the shop. By bedtime there is no room in her own shop for Chen Teh, and she has to go away.

2

Next morning, greatly to the "visitors'" astonishment, the door opens and an extremely hard-looking young business man comes into the shop. He introduces himself as Chen Teh's cousin. Politely but firmly he invites the family to leave the premises, as this is where his cousin must conduct her business. When they prove reluctant to go he promptly summons the police, who gaol one or two of the family's members on some trivial charge. To justify himself to the audience he demonstrates that they were bad people: certain of the sacks which the family has left behind contain opium. – The friendly relations that have grown up between the cousin and the police bear fruit at once. A grateful policeman draws his attention to the flattering interest being taken in his pretty cousin by the prosperous barber Chu Fu from across the way. He is prepared to help set up an assignation in the public park. The cousin expresses interest: Chen Teh is clearly incompetent to run the shop without some protection, and he himself has to go off again and will probably not be able to come back.

3

We see Chen Teh in the park on her way to her assignation with the wealthy barber. Under a tree she sees, to her horror, a down-at-heel young man about to hang himself. He tells her that he is an unemployed pilot and is unable to raise the $500 needed to get him a pilot's job in Peking. A shower of rain forces Chen Teh to take shelter under his tree. A tender conversation ensues. For the first time Chen Teh samples the joy of a man-woman relationship unclouded by material interests. And before she goes home she has promised the pilot to help him get the Peking job. She thinks her cousin may be able to provide the $500. Radiant with joy, she tells her confidant the water seller that in setting out to meet a man who might be able to help her she met a man she is able to help.

Interlude

Before the eyes of the audience Chen Teh transforms herself into her cousin Chui Ta. As she sings a song to explain how impossible it is to perform good deeds without toughness and force she is meantime donning costume and mask of the evil Chui Ta.

4

Chen Teh has asked her friend, the pilot Sun, to come to her shop. In place of the girl he finds her cousin Chui Ta. The latter says he is prepared to provide the $500 for the Peking job, which he reckons a sound financial basis for Sun and Chen Teh. He has asked Mi Tzu to come, a lady tobacco wholesaler who at once offers $300 for the shop. Since Sun evidently has no hesitations the deal is soon agreed. He is radiant as he pockets the $300. Admittedly there is the problem of finding the remaining $200. The cousin's somewhat unscrupulous solution is to make money from the opium which the family of eight have left behind in Chen Teh's shop. Picture his horror, however, not to mention astonishment, when it emerges as a result of a more or less accidental question that the pilot is not thinking of taking the girl to Peking with him. He of course breaks off all further negotiations. The pilot is not so easily dealt with. Not only does he fail to return the $300 he has been given, but he also expresses himself easily confident of getting the balance from the girl, since she is blindly obsessed with him. Triumphantly he leaves the shop in order to wait for her outside. Chui Ta, whom anger and despair have driven to distraction, sends for Chu Fu the barber and tells him that his cousin's unbridled goodness has been the ruin of her, so that she needs a powerful patron right away. The infatuated barber is prepared to discuss the young lady's problems 'over a small supper for two.' As Chui Ta goes off 'to notify his cousin' the pilot Sun smells trouble and reappears in the shop. When Chen Teh emerges from the back room for her outing with the barber she is confronted by Sun. He reminds her of their love; he recalls that wet evening in the park where they first met. Poor Chen Teh! All that Chui Ta has found out about the pilot's bare-faced egotism is washed away by Chen Teh's feelings of love. She leaves, not with the barber her clever cousin has designated, but with the man she loves.

5

At first light, following a night of love, a happy Chen Teh is discovered outside a local teahouse. She is carrying a small sack of opium which she proposes to sell so as to raise the extra $200 needed to get her flier flying. In a kind of mime to musical accompaniment she and we see the opium smokers leaving the teahouse after a night of indulgence, lonely, stumbling, ravaged, and shivering. The sight of these wrecks brings her to her senses. She is quite incapable of buying happiness for herself by trafficking in such deadly poison. Sun will surely understand. He won't reject her if she comes back to him empty-handed. Charged with this hope she hastens away.

6

Chen Teh's hope has not been fulfilled. Sun has left her. In low dives he is drinking all the money raised by the sale of the shop. We next see Chen Teh in the yard, loading her few possessions on a cart. She has lost her little shop, gift of the gods. As she takes down her washing she becomes giddy, and a woman neighbour remarks mockingly that her fine upstanding lover has no doubt put her in the family way. The discovery fills Chen Teh with indescribable joy. She hails the pilot's son as a pilot of the future. Turning round, she can scarcely believe her eyes when she sees a neighbour's child fishing for scraps of food in the dustbin; it is hungry. The sight brings about a complete transformation in her. She makes a big speech to the audience proclaiming her determination to turn herself into a tigress for the sake of the child in her womb. That, it seems to her, is the only way to shield it from poverty and degeneracy. The only one who can help is her cousin.

Interlude

The water seller asks the audience whether they have seen Chen Teh. It is now five months since she vanished. Her cousin has grown rich and is now known as the Tobacco King. Rumour however has it that his prosperity is due to shady dealings. The water seller is sure he is pushing opium.

7

The Tobacco King, Chui Ta, is sitting in solitude in Chen Teh's old but newly smartened-up shop. He has grown fat. Only his housekeeper knows why. The autumn rain seems to make him incline to melancholy. The housekeeper pokes fun at him. Is the master perhaps thinking about that rainy evening in the park? Is he still waiting for the pilot to reappear? The shop door opens and a decrepit individual comes in; it is Sun. Chui Ta is greatly agitated and asks what he can do for him. The ex-pilot brusquely refuses food and clothing. He wants just one thing: opium. Chui Ta, seeing in this unforgotten lover a victim of his own shady traffic, has just begged him to give up this suicidal vice when Wang the water seller appears with his regular monthly enquiry as to the whereabouts of Chen Teh. Reproachfully he informs Chui Ta that she herself told him she was pregnant, and swears that Chen Teh's friends are never going to give up enquiring about her, for good people are both rare and desperately needed. This is too much for Chui Ta. Without a word he goes into the back room. Sun has overheard that Chen Teh is expecting a child. He at once sees an opening for blackmail. Then he hears sobs from the back room; undoubtedly it is Chen Teh's voice. When Chui Ta reenters the shop Sun once again demands opium, and because Chui Ta refuses he goes off uttering threats. Chui Ta's secret is on the verge of being discovered. He must get away. He is just leaving the shop and Szechwan when Sun comes back with the police. A quick search reveals Chen Teh's clothing. The Tobacco King is taken away on suspicion of murder.

8

The water seller has a dream. The three gods appear to him and ask about Chen Teh. He is forced to tell them that she has been murdered by her cousin. The gods are appalled. During their entire trip across the province they failed to find a single other good person. They will return at once.

9

At the trial of Chui Ta the Tobacco King, which has aroused the entire neighbourhood, the three gods appear as judges. As it proceeds Chen Teh's good works are universally lauded and Chui Ta's misdeeds condemned. Chui Ta is forced to justify his harshness by his desire to help his unworldly cousin. He regards himself as her one genuinely disinterested friend. Asked where she is staying at that moment, he has no answer. When cornered he promises to make a statement if the court can be cleared. Once again with his judges he takes off his disguise: he is Chen Teh. The gods are horrified. The one good person they found is the most detested man in the entire city. It can't be true. Incapable of facing this reality they send for a pink cloud and hastily mount it in order to journey back up to their heaven. Chen Teh falls on her knees, imploring them for help and advice. 'How can I be good and yet survive without my cousin, Enlightened Ones?' – 'Well, do your best' is the gods' embarrassed answer. – 'But I've got to have my cousin, Enlightened Ones!' – 'Once a month, that will do.' And despairingly she watches her gods disappear into the sky, waving and smiling.

When the court doors are once again opened the crowd delightedly hails the return of the good person of Szechwan.

[From Werner Hecht (ed.): *Materialien zu Brechts 'Der gute Mensch von Sezuan,'* Frankfurt, Suhrkamp, 1968, pp. 100–106. This outline, doubtless made for Kurt Weill, corresponds to the 'Santa Monica 1943' version of the play, as discussed below, pp. 132 ff.]

ALTERNATIVE EPILOGUE

This Szechwan, as you must have understood
In which one can't survive and still be good
Has gone for ever. It had to disappear.
Yet cities can be found much nearer here
Where doing good can be the end of you
While evil actions help you to win through.
Dear audience, if you live in such a town
Make sure it's changed before it gets you down.
Earth has no happiness that can compare
With freedom to do good while you are there.

[Written about 1953. From Jan Knopf (ed.): *Brechts Guter Mensch von Sezuan.* Suhrkamp, Frankfurt, 1982.]

Editorial Notes

1. DEVELOPMENT OF THE FIRST IDEA

It was not till the spring of 1939, around the time of the German annexation of Czechoslovakia, that Brecht began a serious attempt to write this play which he had been ruminating for so many years. Locating it for the first time clearly in China, and already calling it by its final title, he outlined first a five-scene, then an eight-scene plan, the second of which goes:

> Prologue
> 1. The whore gets a tobacco shop.
> 2. Her cousin has to rescue it.
> 3. The whore falls in love.
> 4. The cousin has to foot the bill.
> 5. The whore's one friend.
> 6. The whore's marriage.
> 7. Suspicion
> 8. Trial

But soon this simple plot grew too elaborate, the cousin's personality too simply bad, the whole play much too long. From Brecht's journal it sounds as if such writing as got done that summer was patchy, and certainly no complete script of this version is known to have survived. It looks as though there was to have been a subsequently eliminated character called Feh Pung, a large-scale tobacco merchant who wished to squeeze the heroine and other small traders out of business; nor did either the landlady or the family of eight figure in the story, the former being replaced by a male landlord, while in lieu of the latter the two prostitutes of scene 2 had a more elaborate role. The barber, for his part, would have been rather more likeable, since he was to have helped the heroine combat the tobacco merchant. The names all through differed from those in our version and were changed at a relatively late stage. Thus Shen Teh/Shui Ta was Li Gung/Lao Go; the pilot Yu Schan or Schan Yu; the water-seller Sun; Mrs Shin at first Mrs Si; and the barber Kau or Kiau. Finally in September, at the time of the German invasion of Poland and the allied declaration of war, the work ground to a halt. Within a fortnight of summing it all up in the 'Press Report' printed on pp. 113 ff., Brecht was hard at work on *Mother Courage* instead.

2. THE FINLAND VERSION

He picked up the threads again the next spring, after moving to Finland in April 1940. 'No play has ever given me so much trouble', he noted in June after he and Margarete Steffin had been working on it concentratedly for some six weeks:

> the material presented many difficulties, and in the (roughly) ten years since i first tackled it i made several false starts.
> the main danger was of being over-schematic. li gung had to be a person if she was to become a good person. as a result her goodness is not of a conventional kind; she is not wholly and invariably good, not even when she is being li gung. nor is lao go conventionally bad, etc. the continual fusion and dissolution of the two characters, and so on, comes off reasonably well, i think. the god's great experiment of extending love of one's neighbour to embrace love of one's self, adding 'be good to thyself' to 'be good to others,' needed to stand apart from the story and at the same time to dominate it . . .

The first complete script in the Brecht Archive dates from this period, but as it is one of Brecht's characteristic pasted-up typescripts, with many later additions and corrections stuck in and yet others written in by hand, much detective work will be needed before we know just what stages it went through. Originally the characters bore the earlier names (apart from Mrs. Si, who had already become Mrs. Shin), which Brecht at some point amended by hand. His journal suggests that this change was decided between August 9 and September 6, 1940, in other words at the last moment before he moved on to intensive work on *Puntila*. However, the addition of the three songs 'Song of the Smoke,' 'Song of the Eighth Elephant,' and 'Trio of the Vanishing Gods on their Cloud,' which were written in January 1941, suggest that the final amendments were probably made during that month. Thereafter it was re-typed and mimeographed, copies being sent to Switzerland, Sweden, and the U.S., with the text virtually as we now have it. Until the 1950s the play bore a dedication to Helene Weigel, Brecht's wife.

The most elaborate of the 'working schemes' used for the play is reproduced on pp.116-7. Its pencilled additions include Li Gung's 'Praise of the Rain' in scene 3 (possibly the origin of the water seller's song on p. 35) and a sketch for the 'Song of the Defenceless of the Good and the Gods' (p. 48 f.). The January revision too seems to have been concerned (to judge from a journal entry of the 25th) with 'introducing a poetic element, a few verses and songs. this should make it lighter and less tedious, even if it cannot be shortened. ' Besides this variation of its texture and the changing of the names it seems that Brecht's reworking of the draft completed the previous June concentrated on four main points: the treatment of the stocks of raw tobacco brought in by the family of eight, the exact details of Shen Teh's borrowings and payments, the direct addressing of the audience, and minor questions of local colour: e.g., should the characters feed on bread and milk or on rice and tea? 'i have taken care to avoid any element of folklore,' he noted at one point. 'on the other hand i don't want people to make a joke of yellow men eating white french bread . . . that would be using china as a mere disguise, and a ragged disguise at that.' What he was striving for rather, he said, was something equivalent to the imaginary London of *The Threepenny Opera* or the Kiplingesque Kilkoa of *Man equals Man*, both of which he considered successful 'poetic conceptions.'

3. ACCOUNT OF THE FIRST SCRIPT

To resume this 1940–41 script scene by scene, the chief points of interest are:

Prologue

Dated by Brecht June 11, 1940 and followed by a photograph of a Chinese water carrier.

1

Here as elsewhere the rice distributed by Shen Teh was originally milk. Sacks of tobacco are brought in by the 'elderly couple' on p. 13, also by the grandfather and the niece. The 'Song of the Smoke' (p. 19) was inserted with the title 'Song of the impoverished family.' The verse 'They are bad' was likewise a later addition (p. 15).

2

The details of Mrs. Mi Tzu's demand for the rent in advance (p. 28) were added to the script, as was the passage with the old woman (p. 30). All sums were originally in yen, not silver dollars.

3

At the start Brecht cut eleven lines in which young prostitute told Shen Teh that her family had seven sacks of tobacco with which to restart in business, and asked her to look after them. Thereafter the rain, Shen

Teh's references to her tame crane, her speech beginning 'There are still friendly people' (p. 36) and the verses 'In our country' (p. 34) and 'How rich I am' (p. 35) were all later additions to the script. The verse 'Hardly was a shelter' in the ensuing interlude (p. 39) was originally at the end of scene 1, where it was spoken by Shen Teh.

4

The episode where the two old people lend Shen Teh the rent money (pp. 43 f.) was certainly reworked, if not actually added to the script. The passage where Shen Teh hands the money to Mrs. Yang, proposes to sell her tobacco stocks and wonders how to raise a further $300 (from 'Of course you can have those now' to 'a pilot has got to fly, that is obvious' on p. 47) appears to be an addition too.

5

In various schemes for the complex finances of this scene it appears that Mrs. Mi Tzu was to buy not only the shop but also the sacks of tobacco left by the family of eight, who would then be reluctant to claim them. This was cut on the script. Brecht also deleted an appearance of the old woman early in the scene to inquire about her loan, substituting instead the exchange between Sun and Shui Ta (p. 52); both versions stress that there was no agreement in writing. Notes made after the change of names show Brecht concenred to reconcile Sun's more 'hooligan-like' features with his genuine keenness for flying. At that stage his boasting about his hold over Shen Teh was primarily intended to impress Mrs. Mi Tzu, not (as now) Shui Ta. The barber, too, was at this point to suggest turning his empty houses into a tobacco factory for the general benefit of the neighbourhood.

6

Brecht added Sun's references to the 'gremlins' (p. 63 f.) and the mention of the odd couple (on p. 65). Shen Teh's demand that Sun repay the $200 is not in this script, and only appears in that of the Zurich production.

7

The first six lines, with their further mention of repayment, are not in the script. Shu Fu's gift of the blank cheque (p. 72) is not in the working plan, and it appears that the whole ending of the scene, with its installation of the factory in Shu Fu's sheds, was extensively worked over. Previously this development was to have been left to scene 8, while the sacks (subsequently bales) of tobacco would already have been sold in scene 5. The script specifies that Shen Teh's big verse speech on p. 37 should be accompanied by the music of the 'Song of the Defencelessness of the Good and the Gods', which would continue softly after its end. Her little rhyme about 'A plum off my tree' (p. 74) was added in revision.

8

Though the scene is dated May 21, 1940, the 'Song of the Eighth Elephant' (p. 87) was added in January. Most of the indications that Mrs. Yang's remarks were to be addressed to the audience were likewise additions.

9

Bears the dates May 23 and June 17 and seems to have been scarcely revised since.

10

Dated Helsingfors, May 29 and June 17, 1940, but bears signs of considerable subsequent reworking. Shen Teh's big speech (pp. 105 ff.) looks like a separate insertion, and the reference to her as 'strong, healthy and well-built' (p. 106) is added in Brecht's hand. Originally on this script the scene ended with 'Once a month: that will be enough' (p. 108), followed by the final quatrain. The gods' trio, initially with a slightly different first verse, was added in the January revision.

The epilogue is not included in this script, whose finally amended version is otherwise to all intents and purposes the same as the final text used in our edition.

4. THE ZURICH SCRIPT OF 1943

For the play's first production at the Zurich Schauspielhaus a duplicated script was made by the Reiss-Verlag of Basel. Sub-titled 'A Parable by Bertold Brecht', this again is very close to the final text, but includes a number of small dramaturgical changes due presumably to the theatre. Thus it runs most of the interludes into the immediately preceding scenes, puts an intermission after scene 5 and makes the following cuts:

1

The sacks of tobacco previously brought by the elderly couple were omitted.

6

Cut from Sun's 'Why not?' (p. 63) to the start of Mrs. Yang's next speech (p. 63).

8

Cut stage direction and Mrs. Yang's speech, following the song.

9

Cut from 'SHUI TA *pitifully*' to '*in Mrs. Shin's arms*' (p. 89), also the stage direction and Wang's first speech in the interlude following.

10

Cut from 'Mr Shui Ta, on the other hand' to 'from straight perjury'. (pp. 100–101). Again, there was no epilogue.

5. THE SANTA MONICA VERSION

Even before the Zurich production Brecht had tried to arouse interest in the play in the U.S., but without yet attempting to modify it for the very different audience there. It was only later, when Kurt Weill thought he might be able to arrange a Broadway production, that Brecht in New York hurriedly made what he termed 'a szechwan version for here.' Though this has not been firmly identified, it could well be the 'story' printed on p. 121 ff., which was found inside one of the duplicated copies of the Finnish version, from which however it differs extensively. The full script embodying this story, typed by Brecht himself and marked 'only copy,' was headed '1943 version' and datelined Santa Monica 1943, so that it must have been written after his return there from New York at the end of May, probably once the main work on *Schweyk* had been completed. By September 20 Brecht's journal shows that Christopher Isherwood had read the play but was not interested enough to want to translate it as its author had hoped. Thereafter, as Weill began to think rather of making a 'semi-opera' of it, the new script was set aside and apparently forgotten, subsequent U.S. translations and productions being based, so far as we know, on the previous version. This seems surprising in view of Brecht's success not only in shortening and simplifying the play but also in shedding a more critical light on the heroine's goodness, and thus interweaving the ideas of good and evil as he wanted in the earlier journal entry printed on p. 128. The principal differences from our text are as follows:

Prologue

As before.

1

The stage direction for the entry of the elderly couple on p. 13 adds '*The wife and the shabbily dressed man are carrying sacks on their shoulders.*' Then there is a long cut from Mrs. Mi Tzu's entry (p. 17) to the nephew's 'Over the shelving' (p. 18), after which the former's exit speech, starting 'Well, I shall also be glad', and the wife's ensuing comment, ending 'all about you by the morning,' (p. 18) are likewise cut.

2

Unchanged up to where Shui Ta bows (p. 27). Thereafter the rest of the scene is different, thus:

SHUI TA: There's just one thing: aren't you going to take your sacks?

THE HUSBAND, *giving him a conspiratorial look*: What sacks? You know we didn't bring any sacks with us.

SHUI TA, *slowly*: Oh. Then either my cousin got it wrong or I must have misunderstood her. *To the policeman*: It's quite all right.

THE POLICEMAN: Get going, you! *he drives them out.*

THE GRANDFATHER, *solemnly, from the doorway*: Good morning.
    Exit all, except Shui Ta.
    Shui Ta hastens backstage and brings out a sack.

SHUI TA, *showing the sack to the audience*: Opium! *He hears somebody approaching and quickly hides the sack.*

THE POLICEMAN, *reentering*: I've handed those crooks over to my colleague. Forgive my coming back. I would like to thank you in the name of the police.

SHUI TA: It is for me to thank you, officer.

THE POLICEMAN, *negligently*: You were saying something about sacks. Did those crooks leave anything here, Mr. Shui Ta?

SHUI TA: Not a button. Do you smoke?

THE POLICEMAN, *putting two cigars in his pocket*: Mr. Shui Ta, I must admit we at the station began by viewing this shop with mixed feelings, but your decisive action on the side of the law just now showed us the sort of man you are. We don't take long to find out who can be relied on as a friend of law and order. I only hope you will be staying here.

SHUI TA: Unfortunately I shall not be staying here and I cannot come again. I was able to give my cousin a hand just because I was passing through; I merely saved her from the worst. Any minute now she will be thrown back on her own resources. I am worried as to what will happen.

THE POLICEMAN: All you have to do is find a husband for her.

SHUI TA: A husband?

THE POLICEMAN, *eagerly*: Why not? She's a good match. Between you and me and the doorpost I had a hint only yesterday from Mr. Shu Fu, the barber next door, that he is taking a flattering interest in the young lady, and he's a gentleman who owns twelve houses and has only one wife and an old one at that. He went so far as to ask about her financial standing. That shows real affection . . .

SHUI TA, *cautiously*: It's not a bad idea. Could you arrange a meeting?

THE POLICEMAN: I think so. It would have to be done delicately, of course. Mr. Shu Fu is very sensitive. I'd say, an accidental meeting outside the teahouse by the city lake. There's a bath-hut there; I know because I had the good fortune to make an arrest there last week. Miss Shen Teh should be looking at the goldfish and in her delight could let drop some remark such as . . . well, what?

SHUI TA: Look at the pretty goldfish.

THE POLICEMAN: Brilliant. And Mr. Shu Fu could reply, let's say, for example . . .

SHUI TA: All I can see is a pretty face mirrored in the water, madam.

THE POLICEMAN: Perfect. I'll speak to Mr. Shu Fu at once. Don't think, Mr. Shui Ta, that the authorities have no sympathy for the honest businessman.

SHUI TA: Indeed I foresaw a black outlook for this little shop which my cousin regards as a gift of the gods. But now I see a way out. It is almost frightening how much luck one needs in order to live, what brilliant ideas, what good friends.

3

Up to p. 35 f. the first two-thirds of the scene are unchanged, except that on p. 32 and again on p. 35 Shen Teh 'has got' to marry the man she is meeting at the teahouse, not merely 'is going' to. Then from 'Have you got a friend?' at the end of Sun's speech (p. 35) to Shen Teh's 'And that was a raindrop' (p. 36) there is a cut and the following is substituted:

SHEN TEH: They say that to speak without hope is to speak without kindness.
SUN: I have no hope. I need 500 dollars to be human. This morning when a letter came saying there was a job for me the first thing I did was to get myself a rope; you see, it costs 500 dollars.
SHEN TEH: It's a flier's job? *He nods, and she slowly goes on.* I have a friend, a cousin of mine, who might be able to raise that amount. This friend is too cunning and hard. It really would have to be the last time. But a flier must fly, that's obvious.
SUN: What do you think you are talking about?
SHEN TEH: Please come tomorrow to Sandalmakers' Street. You'll find a small tobacco shop. If I'm not there my cousin will be.
SUN, *laughs*: And if your cousin isn't there nobody will be, is that it? *He looks at her.* Your shawl's really the prettiest thing about you.
SHEN TEH: Yes? *Pause.* And now I've felt a raindrop.

And so on as in our text, up to the end of the poem on p. 37. The scene then finishes thus:

WANG: Weren't you meeting somebody in the park who was going to be able to help you?
SHEN TEH: Yes, but now I've found somebody I am going to be able to help, Wang.

After that come the stage direction (*She pays . . .*) and her last laughing remark to Wang as we have them.

4

Is omitted, only the first six lines from Shen Teh's monologue about the city (p. 42) being kept and transposed to a new interlude before scene 7.
  The interlude before the curtain which follows remains unchanged.

5

Instead of as on p. 49 Mrs. Shin's first speech reads:

MRS. SHIN: I may be an old gossip, Mr. Shui Ta, but I think you should know what's going on. Once people start talking about how Miss Shen Teh never comes home before morning – and you know we have all the scum of the district hanging round the shop at crack of dawn to get a plate of rice – then a shop like this gets a bad name, and where do you go from there?

On page 49 for Sun's 'Oh boy. I'm going to be flying again' substitute 'Neat, very neat.' For 300 dollars (three times) read 500. For the two lines 'it was good of her' to 'or I'm stuck' read 'Nothing for it, we'll have to sell.' Then omit Shui Ta's next two sentences, (from 'Perhaps' to 'her business'), and for Sun's 'All to her credit of course' below substitute 'Really.' About a page further on delete Shui Ta's sentence about the 200 dollars and the rent, and for both mentions of 250 dollars (amount of Sun's pay in Peking) substitute 150 dollars. In Shui Ta's next speech, for 'the landlady' (p. 51) substitute 'the lady tobacco merchant' (*Tabakhändlerin*). The dialogue from that point reads:

THE LADY TOBACCO MERCHANT, *enters*: Good morning, Mr. Shui Ta. Are you really wanting to sell the shop?

SHUI TA: Mrs. Mi Tzu, my cousin is contemplating marriage, and her future husband – *he introduces Yang Sun* – Mr. Yang Sun, is taking her to Peking where they wish to start a new life. If I can get a good price for my tobacco I shall sell it.

THE LADY TOBACCO MERCHANT: How much do you need?

SHUI TA: 500 in cash.

THE LADY TOBACCO MERCHANT: How much did your stock cost?

SHUI TA: My cousin originally paid 1000 silver dollars, and very little of it has been sold.

THE LADY TOBACCO MERCHANT: 1000 silver dollars! She was swindled of course. I'll make you an offer: you can have 300 silver dollars for the whole business, if you move out the day after tomorrow.

SUN: All right. That's it, old boy!

SHUI TA: It's too little.

SUN: We'd consider that, certainly, but 300 isn't enough. *Like an auctioneer*. First-class tobacco, recently acquired, in admirable condition, price 1000 dollars F.O.B. Together with complete shop fittings and a growing clientèle, attracted by the good looks of the proprietress. The whole to be knocked down for only 500 dollars due to special circumstances. It's an opportunity that mustn't be missed. Now you're an intelligent woman, you know what life's about, it's written all over you. *He strokes her*. You know what love is, it's plain to see. The shop's got to go, selling below cost price due to hasty marriage – the sort of chance that occurs once in a business lifetime.

THE LADY TOBACCO MERCHANT, *not unaffected, but still firmly*: 300 dollars.

SUN, *with a sidelong glance at Shui Ta*: Not enough, but better than nothing, what? 300 in hand would give us room to turn around in.

SHUI TA, *alarmed*: But 300 won't get us the job.

SUN: OK, but what good is a shop to me?

SHUI TA: But everything would have gone, there'd be nothing to live on.

SUN: But I'd have the 300 dollars. *To the lady tobacco merchant.* It's a deal. Lock, stock, and barrel for 300 dollars, and our troubles are over. How soon can we have the 300?

THE LADY TOBACCO MERCHANT: Right away. *She pulls notes from her bag.* Here, 300 dollars, and that's because I'm glad to help where it seems to be a case of young love.

SUN, *to Shui Ta*: Write down 300 on the contract. Shen Teh's signature's already on it, I see.

Shui Ta fills in the figure and hands the contract to the lady tobacco merchant. Sun takes the notes away from him.

THE LADY TOBACCO MERCHANT: Good-bye, Mr. Yang Sun; good-bye, Mr. Shui Ta. Please remember me to Miss Shen Teh. *Goes out.*

SUN, *sits down exhausted on the counter*: We've made it, old boy.

SHUI TA: But it's not enough.

SUN: That's right. We need another 200. You'll have to find them.

SHUI TA: How am I to do that without stealing?

SUN: Your cousin certainly thought you were the right man to find them.

SHUI TA: Perhaps I am. *Slowly.* I took it that the point at issue was Shen Teh's happiness. A person's goodness, they said, doesn't have to be denied to that person and the same applies to his or her compassion.

SUN: Right, partner. O boy, I'm going to be flying again!

SHUI TA, *smiling and with a bow*: A flier has to fly. *Negligently.* Have you got the money for both your tickets, and enough to tide you over?

Thereafter the dialogue continues as we have it from Sun's 'Sure' (p. 52) to the *Pause* on p. 53. Then Shui Ta continues:

I should like you to hand me back the 300 dollars, Mr. Yang Sun, and leave them in my custody until you are able to show me two tickets to Peking.

SUN: Why? You mean you don't trust me?

SHUI TA: I don't trust anybody.

SUN: Why specially me?

They look at each other.

SUN: My dear brother-in-law, I would prefer it if you didn't meddle in the intimate affairs of people in love. We don't understand one another, I see. As for the other 200 I'll have to rely on the girl.

SHUI TA, *incredulously*: Do you really expect her to give up everything for you if you aren't even thinking of taking her along?

SUN: She will. Even so.

SHUI TA: And you are not afraid of what I might have to say against it?

Then back to our text from Sun's 'My dear man' (p. 53), but with the following modifications. First of all Sun's exit speech (pp. 53-54) ends after *puts the box under his arm*'.

> And now I'm going to go and wait outside the shop, and don't let it worry you if we're a bit late tonight. We're having supper together and we'll be talking about that missing 200.

Then Mrs. Shin's second sentence 'And the whole Yellow Alley' is cut, as is her speech following the poem (p. 54). Instead Shen Teh concludes the poem by saying 'Fetch Mr. Shu Fu the barber at once,' and Shin '*dashes off*'. About a page later there is a long cut from Wang's entry with the policeman (p. 55) to immediately before Shui Ta's 'I shall hasten to inform my cousin' (p. 57). Roughly two pages after that, Sun's 'But I can put up a light' (p. 59) is followed by a new insertion 'Look me in the eyes. Do you really believe I can't be in love with you without a dowry?' before continuing 'They're wrecking' and so on as in our text. Finally, after Shen Teh's 'I want to go away with Sun' (p. 59) Sun says 'Bring your shawl, the blue one,' and '*Shen Teh fetches the shawl she wore in the park*' before Sun goes on 'We are in love, you know' and so on to the end.

The ensuing interlude (p. 60) is partly absorbed in the new interlude outside a teahouse (see below).

6

Is omitted, as is the interlude (pp. 69-71) which follows it.

Interlude Outside a Teahouse

This is mainly new. Carrying a small sack, Shen Teh addresses the audience as at the beginning of our scene 4 (p. 41), from 'I had never seen the city at dawn', but omitting the sentence 'It was a long walk' etc. After 'filling his lungs with fresh air and reaching for his tools' (p. 42) she continues:

And here is the Teahouse of Bliss where I am supposed to sell this little sack so that Sun may fly again. *She tries to enter, but guests are leaving. They are opium smokers, human wrecks, stumbling and freezing. A young man takes out his purse, finds it empty and throws it away. A hideous old woman escorts a very young drugged girl.* That's terrible. It's opium that has ruined them like that. *She looks at her sack in horror.* It's poison. How could I think of selling this? It doesn't even belong to me. How could I forget that too?

Then she goes into the monologue on p. 60, starting at 'In the tumult of my feelings', omitting the sentence 'How could I simply have forgotten two good old people?' and ending after 'he will understand' (p. 60) with:

He would rather get a job at the cement works than owe his flying to a filthy deal. I must go to him at once.

7 [renumbered 6]

After the opening stage direction, which is as in our text, Mrs. Shin's speech is changed to read: 'There you are, your shop's gone and the whole district knows that for weeks that pilot of yours has been boozing away the money in the lowest sort of bar.' Shen Teh *says nothing.* Then Shin continues 'All gone, eh' as in our text (p. 31), down to Shen Teh's 'earn a bit as a tobacco sorter?' Then:

A child appears in the gateway to the yard.

MRS. SHIN, *shooing it away:* Clear out, you! *To Shen Teh:* Those gutter vultures only need to get one sniff of bankruptcy and before you know it they come around stuffing their pockets.

SHEN TEH: Oh, let him look through my junk. He might find something worth taking.

MRS. SHIN: If there's anything worth taking I'm taking it. You haven't paid me for the washing yet. Beat it or I'll call the police! *Child disappears.*

Shen Teh then asks 'Why are you so unpleasant?' introducing the poem as on p. 75. After it Mrs. Shin comments 'A pity your cousin didn't hear that,' and goes on 'What are Mr Shui Ta's trousers doing here?' etc., as on p. 71. After Shen Teh's 'No' seven lines further on there is another new passage:

Lin To the carpenter appears in the gateway.

THE CARPENTER: Good morning, Miss Shen Teh. There's a story going round the district that you have got permission for the homeless to move into Shu Fu the barber's houses. Is that right?

MRS. SHIN: It was right. But now we've given Shu Fu the brushoff there ain't going to be no accommodation.

THE CARPENTER: That's a pity. I don't know what I can do with my family.

MRS. SHIN: It looks as if Miss Shen Teh will be in the happy position of being able to ask *you* for accommodation. *The carpenter goes out, disappointed.* There'll be a lot more of them coming along.

SHEN TEH: This is dreadful.

MRS. SHIN: You think you're too good for the barber, so the plague huts down by the river are going to have to be good enough for Lin To and his family. If you ask me you're not giving up that pilot of yours in spite of the bad way he has behaved to you. Don't you mind him being such a bad person?

SHEN TEH: It all comes from poverty.

Then she addresses the poem to the audience as on pp. 72-73, after which the text continues, with one exception, as we have it until after the plum rhyme that ends her big speech (p. 74). The exception is that the mention of the barber's cheque is cut; thus after Mrs. Shin's 'Let's only hope it isn't a little one' (p. 73) the speaker *laughs* and continues: 'Your pilot has fixed you good and proper. Landed you with a kid, that's what he's done!' Then *She goes to the rear* and so on. But once past the plum rhyme this version is different:

> *The child reappears in the gateway. It seems surprised by Shen Teh's play-acting. Suddenly she observes it and beckons it into the yard.*

THE CHILD: Where are you going?

SHEN TEH: I don't know, Ni Tzu.

The child rubs its stomach and looks expectantly at her.

SHEN TEH: I haven't any more rice, Ni Tzu, not a grain.

THE CHILD: Don't go.

SHEN TEH: I'd like to stay.

> *The water seller is heard calling 'Buy water!'*

SHEN TEH: That's something I can still do for you. Come on, little man. *To the audience.*

Hey, you people. Someone is asking for shelter.
A citizen of tomorrow is asking you for a today.

> *To the child*: Wait a moment. *She hurries to the gateway, where the water seller has appeared.*

WANG: Good morning, Shen Teh. Is it true that you're having to clear out of your shop?

SHEN TEH: That's not important: happiness has come to me, I am to have a child, Wang. I'm so glad you came; I had to tell somebody about it. But don't repeat that or Yang Sun may hear of it, and he won't want us. Give me a cupful.

He gives her a cup of water. When she turns round with it she sees the child and stiffens. It has gone over to the dustbin and is fishing around in it. It picks out something which it eats.

SHEN TEH, *to Wang:* Please go at once; I'm not well. *She pushes him out.* He's hungry. Fishing in the garbage.

Then *She lifts up the child* (p. 77) and makes her big verse speech as in our text, and the scene ends with 'for the last time, I hope' on p. 78.

A new, much shorter interlude follows in lieu of the present one (p. 82). It goes thus:

The water seller walks slowly along before the curtain as if it were a street. He stops and addresses the audience.

WANG: Can any of you good people tell me where to find Miss Shen Teh, formerly of Sandalmakers' Street. It's five months since she completely vanished. That was when her cousin suddenly popped up – must have been for the third time – what's more [?] there have been some queer business dealings in her tobacco shop, very profitable but dirty. *Softly.* Opium. The worst of it is I'm no longer in touch with the Enlightened Ones. It may be because I'm so worried I can't sleep a wink, so that I no longer have dreams. Anyway, if you do see Shen Teh, could you tell her to get in touch with me? We miss her badly in our district; she is such a good person, you see. *He walks worriedly on.*

8

Is omitted.

9 [renumbered 7]

This is the scene in Shen Teh's shop (pp. 88 ff.), but with changes. It starts thus:

The shop has been transformed into an office, with easy chairs and fine carpets. Shui Ta, fat and expensively dressed, is ushering out the elderly couple and the nephew who called on Shen Teh the day the shop was opened. Mrs. Shin, in noticeably new clothes, is watching with amusement. Outside it is raining.

SHUI TA: I tell you for the tenth time I never found any sacks in the back room.

THE WIFE: Then we'd better write to Miss Shen Teh. What's her address?

SHUI TA: I'm afraid I don't know.

THE NEPHEW: So that's it. The sacks have gone, but you've done all right for yourself.

SHUI TA: That indeed is it.

MRS. SHIN: Better watch your step. Mr. Shui Ta found jobs in his factory for some of your family, didn't he? His patience might suddenly give out.

THE WIFE: But the work's ruining my boy's health. It's more than he can take.

Shui Ta shrugs his shoulders. The elderly couple and the nephew go off angrily.

SHUI TA, *feebly*: Working in a factory unhealthy? Work's work.

MRS. SHIN: Those people wouldn't have got anywhere with their couple of sacks. That sort of thing is just a foundation, and it takes very special talents to build any real prosperity on it. *You* have them.

SHUI TA, *has to sit down because he feels sick*: I feel dizzy again.

MRS. SHIN, *bustling around him*: You're six months gone! You mustn't let yourself get worked up. Lucky for you you've got me. All of us can do with a helping hand. Yes, when your time comes I shall be at your side. *She laughs.*

SHEN TEH, *feebly*: Can I count on that, Mrs. Shin?

MRS. SHIN: You bet. It'll cost money, of course.

A smartly dressed man enters. He is the unemployed man who was given cigarettes the day the shop was opened.

THE AGENT: Our accounts, Mr. Shui Ta. From street-corner clients 50 dollars. From the Teahouse of Bliss . . .

SHUI TA, *laboriously*: Go away. Tomorrow.

MRS. SHIN: Can't you see Mr. Shui Ta isn't up to it?

THE AGENT: But we've got a little problem with the police in District Four. One consignment got into the wrong hands, Mr. Shui Ta.

MRS. SHIN: Can't you ever handle anything by yourself?

The agent starts to go, nervously.

SHUI TA: Wait! Hand over the money!

The agent hands over money and goes.

Then as in our text from 'SHUI TA, *pitifully*' down to 'They're watching the shop' (p. 89) after which Mrs. Shin says:

Have a drop of water, dear. *She gets some water.* Why don't you move out of this place and take a villa in a better district? Oh, but I know why. You're still waiting for that broken-down pilot. That's a weakness.

SHUI TA: Nonsense.

Enter a decrepit figure, the former pilot Yang Sun. He is amazed to see Shui Ta in Mrs. Shin's arms, being made to drink by her.

SUN, *hoarsley*: Am I disturbing you?

Shui Ta gets up with difficulty and stares at him.

MRS. SHIN: Mr. Yang Sun in person.

SUN, *respectfully*: Excuse me coming to see you dressed like this, Mr. Shui Ta. My luggage got held up, and I didn't want the rain to stop my calling on one or two of my old acquaintances, you see.

SHUI TA, *draws Mrs. Shin aside before she can open her mouth*: Go and find him some clothes.

MRS. SHIN: Chuck him out right away. I'm telling you.

SHUI TA, *sharply*: You do what you're told. *Mrs. Shin goes out, protesting.*

SUN: Woollen rugs. What riches. I'm told people are calling you the Tobacco King, Mr. Shui Ta.

SHUI TA: I've been lucky.

SUN: Oh, Mr. Shui Ta, it isn't just luck; you've earned it. Ah yes, some get fat and others get thin, that's it, isn't it?

SHUI TA: I take it that fate has not been kind to you, Mr. Yang Sun; but are you ill?

SUN: Me? No, my health is fine.

SHUI TA: Good. Damage to one's health is the only thing that cannot sooner or later be repaired, I would say.

Enter Mrs. Shin from the back room with clothing.

SHUI TA: I hope these things will fit you. Isn't that hat rather big?

Mrs. Shin tries a hat on Sun.

SHUI TA: Yes, it's too big. Get another, Mrs. Shin.

SUN: I don't want a hat. *Suddenly angry.* What are you up to? Trying to buy me off with an old hat? *Controlling himself.* Why should I want your hat? It's something else I need. *Ingratiatingly.* Mr. Shui Ta, would you grant just one favour to a man down on his luck?

SHUI TA: What can I do for you?

MRS. SHIN: It's written all over him. I can tell you what kind of a favour he means.

SHUI TA, *beginning to understand*: No!

MRS. SHIN: Opium, eh?

SHUI TA: Sun!

SUN: Only a little packet, enough for two or three pipes. That's all I need. I don't care about clothes or food. But I've got to have my pipe.

SHUI TA, *in the depths of horror*: Not opium! Don't tell me you're a victim of that vice. Listen to me, those wretches who think it may help them escape their miseries for an hour or two are plunged in misery by it forever, so that in no time they need the drug not to make them happy but simply to reduce their worst sufferings.

SUN: I see you know all about it. That's how it is with me.

SHUI TA: Turn back at once! You must be ruthless and control your craving; never touch the drug again, you can do it.

SUN: All very well for you to say that, Mr. Shui Ta; you deal in it and know all about it. Your livelihood depends on us smokers not finding the way back.

SHUI TA: Water! I feel sick.

MRS. SHIN: You haven't been in form lately, not in your old form. *Mockingly.* Perhaps it's Mr. Yang Sun's fault for bringing the rain with him. Rain always makes you so touchy and melancholic. I expect you know why.

SHUI TA: Go away.

Then Wang's voice is heard singing, as on p. 91, but this time it is Mrs. Shin who comments: 'There's that bloody water-seller. Now he'll be nagging us again'. She then *goes out at a sign from Shui Ta* as his voice continues with his speech *from outside*, after which Sun says, pressingly:

We'll make a bargain. Give me what I asked for, and I'll shut him up. What business is it of his, where she is?

Then Wang enters, and with two minor changes the text is the same as ours up to Shui Ta's 'Have you dropped that?' on p. 93. The first change is the addition of the words '*as if transformed*' after 'SUN, *to the audience*' on p. 92. The second is the substitution seven lines on of 'left here rotting' for 'left here to work like a slave' and the addition of 'So that lousy water seller can't even recognise me' before '*He is losing his temper*'. Then after 'Have you dropped that?' the next four pages of our text are considerably changed and shortened, going on thus:

SUN, *cautiously*: Why do you ask that? Want to buy me a pilot's job? Now? What makes you think anyone can fly with hands like this? *He shows his; they are trembling.* Where's my fiancée? Do you hear me? I said, where is my fiancée Shen Teh?

SHUI TA: Do you really want to know?

SUN: I should think so.

SHUI TA: My cousin might be pleased to hear that.

SUN: Anyway, I'm concerned enough not to be able to shut my eyes if, for instance, I find that she is being deprived of her freedom.

SHUI TA: By whom?

SUN: By you.

Pause.

SHUI TA: What would you do in such an eventuality?

SUN, *crudely*: I'd say you had better meet my request and no arguing about it.

SHUI TA: Your request for . . .

SUN, *hoarsely*: The stuff, of course.

SHUI TA: Aha. *Pause.* Mr. Yang Sun, you will not get a single pinch of that drug out of me.

SUN: In that case perhaps your cousin wouldn't deny the father of her child a few pipes of opium every day and a bench to sleep on? Dear cousin-in-law, my longing for the lady of my heart cannot be suppressed. I feel I shall be forced to take steps if I am to enfold her in my arms once more. *He calls.* Shen Teh! Shen Teh!

SHUI TA: Didn't they tell you Shen Teh has gone away? Do you want to search the back room?

SUN, *giving him a peculiar look*: No, I don't, anyway not by myself. I'm not physically in any condition to fight with you. The police are better fed. *He leaves quickly, taking care not to present his back to Shui Ta.*

Shui Ta looks at him without moving. Then he goes quickly into the back room once more and brings out all kinds of things belonging to Shen Teh: underwear, toilet articles, a dress. He looks lengthily at the shawl which Sun once commented favourably on in the park, then packs it all up in a bundle. Then he gets a suitcase and some men's clothes which he stuffs into it.

SHUI TA, *with the bundle and the suitcase*: So this is the finish. After all my efforts and triumphs I am having to leave this flourishing business which I developed from the dirty little shop thought good enough by the gods. Just one weak moment, one unforseeable attack of softness, and I'm pitched into the abyss. I only had to let that broken-down creature open his mouth, instead of instantly handing him over to the police for having embezzled $300, and I was ruined. No amount of toughness and inhumanity will do unless it is total. That's the kind of world it is.

On hearing sounds from outside, he hurriedly stuffs the bundle under the table. Somebody throws a stone outside the window. Voices of an excited crowd outside. Enter Sun, Wang and the policeman.

The scene then ends virtually as it does after their entry in our text (p. 96). The policeman in his first speech says 'we' instead of 'I' and omits the words 'received from your own firm.' Then in place of Mrs. Mi Tzu's speech Sun *'points at the bundle'* saying, 'He's packed his things. He wanted to clear out.' Finally Shui Ta's last speech is cut and he simply *'bows and goes out ahead of the policeman.'*

The interlude which follows (pp. 98-99) is as we have it.

10 [renumbered 8]

This is very largely the last scene as we have it, less the epilogue. Minor changes in the first part are:

P. 99, for Wang's first speech substitute 'I've collected as many witnesses as I could.'

Three lines below, for 'property owner' substitute 'lady tobacco merchant.'

P. 99 for 'THE OLD WOMAN' substitute 'THE YOUNG PROSTITUTE.'

Pp. 100-101, in the policeman's evidence cut the two sentences beginning 'There were some people' down to 'perjury.' P. 101, Mrs. Mi Tzu's evidence goes:

As president of the United District Charities, I wish to bring to the attention of the court that Mr. Shui Ta is giving bread and work to a considerable number of people in his tobacco factories. This Shen Teh person, by contrast, was not in particularly good repute.

Five lines below, Wang steps forward with *'the carpenter and the family of eight'*.

There are also still slighter changes in the German which would not affect the translation. After the sister-in-law's 'But we had nowhere to go,' however (p. 102), the scene goes on thus:

SHUI TA: There were too many of you. The lifeboat was on the point of capsizing. I got it afloat again. There wasn't a single morning when the poor of the district failed to get their rice. My cousin regarded her shop as a gift of the gods.

WANG: That didn't prevent you from wanting to sell it off.

SHUI TA: Because my cousin was helping an airman to get back into the air again. I was supposed to find the money.

WANG: She may have wanted that, but you had your eye on that good job in Peking. The shop wasn't good enough for you.

SHUI TA: My cousin had no idea of business.

MRS. SHIN: Besides, she was in love with the airman.

SHUI TA: Hadn't she the right to love?

WANG: Of course she had. So why did you try to make her marry a man she didn't love, the barber here?

SHUI TA: The man she loved was a crook.

THE FIRST GOD, *showing interest*: Who was it she was in love with?

MRS. SHIN, *pointing at Sun, who is sitting like some kind of animal*: That's him. They say birds of a feather flock together. So much for the private life of your Angel of the Slums.

WANG: It wasn't the fact that he was like her that made her love him, but the fact that he was miserable. She didn't just help him because she loved him; she also loved him because she helped him.

THE SECOND GOD: You are right. Loving like that was not unworthy of her.

SHUI TA: But it was mortally dangerous.

THE FIRST GOD: Isn't he the one who accused you of her murder?

SUN: Of restricting her freedom. He couldn't have murdered her. A few minutes before the arrest I heard Shen Teh's voice from the room behind the shop.

Then from the first god's '*intrigued*' question (on p. 103) for ten lines, down to Shui Ta's 'Because you didn't love her,' the text is the same as ours, after which:

SUN: I was out of work.

WANG, *to Shui Ta*: You were out for the barber's money, you mean.

SHUI TA: But what was the money needed for, your worships? *To Sun*: You wanted her to sacrifice everything, but the barber offered his buildings and his money so that she could help the poor. Even to let her do good I had to promise her to the barber. But she didn't want that.

Brecht's Plays, Poetry and Prose
annotated and edited in hardback and paperback
by John Willett and Ralph Manheim

Collected Plays

The following plays are also available (in paperback) in unannotated editions:
The Caucasian Chalk Circle; The Days of the Commune; The Life of Galileo; The Measures Taken and other Lehrstücke; The Messingkauf Dialogues; The Mother; Saint Joan of the Stockyards

*in preparation   †not available from Methuen